RESPONDING TO
RESISTANCE

30
STRATEGIES
TO MANAGE
CONFLICT
IN YOUR SCHOOL

WILLIAM A. SOMMERS

Solution Tree | Press

a division of
Solution Tree

555 North Morton Street
Bloomington, IN 47404
800.733.6786 (toll free) / 812.336.7700
FAX: 812.336.7790

email: info@SolutionTree.com
SolutionTree.com

Visit **go.SolutionTree.com/leadership** to download the free reproducibles in this book.

Printed in the United States of America

Names: Sommers, William A., author.
Title: Responding to resistance : thirty strategies to manage conflict in
  your school / William A. Sommers.
Description: Bloomington, IN : Solution Tree Press, [2020] | Includes
  bibliographical references and index.
Identifiers: LCCN 2020014328 (print) | LCCN 2020014329 (ebook) | ISBN
  9781951075057 (paperback) | ISBN 9781951075064 (ebook)
Subjects: LCSH: School management and organization. | Conflict management.
Classification: LCC LB2805 .S725 2020 (print) | LCC LB2805 (ebook) | DDC
  371.2--dc23
LC record available at https://lccn.loc.gov/2020014328
LC ebook record available at https://lccn.loc.gov/2020014329

Solution Tree
Jeffrey C. Jones, CEO
Edmund M. Ackerman, President

Solution Tree Press
President and Publisher: Douglas M. Rife
Associate Publisher: Sarah Payne-Mills
Art Director: Rian Anderson
Managing Production Editor: Kendra Slayton
Production Editor: Laurel Hecker
Content Development Specialist: Amy Rubenstein
Proofreader: Elisabeth Abrams
Text and Cover Designer: Abigail Bowen
Editorial Assistants: Sarah Ludwig and Elijah Oates

ACKNOWLEDGMENTS

No written work is done in isolation. Some of the major influencers for me are the following people, although this is not an exhaustive list. I am grateful for all my teachers and friends who contributed to my knowledge, skills, and applications.

- Diane Zimmerman—my best critical friend and friendly critic. I am eternally grateful for her guidance and support.

- Stevie Ray—my improv teacher who helped me respond better in the day-to-day actions of schools. He is a master presenter and master of improv.

- Solution Tree staff—Douglas Rife, for accepting this proposal. Amy Rubenstein, for giving me immediate feedback on the early drafts. Laurel Hecker, for making this a much better manuscript. Feedback and suggestions were so helpful.

- Ruby Payne—my coauthor on *Living on a Tightrope*. She said about teaching kids in poverty, "Don't scold them or excuse them, teach them." I never forgot this.

- Skip Olsen—as a union business agent, Skip was invaluable giving me advice to do the right thing, the right way. We have collaborated ever since on books, trainings, and thinking.

- Michael Grinder—learning nonverbal communication strengthened my management and presentation skills.

- Bob Garmston—when traveling together in the '90s to do a training I asked Bob, "What are you working on?" He responded, "How to turn negative energy into positive energy."
- Jennifer Abrams—her book *Swimming in the Deep End* inspired me to write this book. She has provided me with many creative conversations about school cultures.

Solution Tree Press would like to thank the following reviewers:

Morgan Freeck
Instructional Specialist
Elmwood Park Community
  Unit School District 401
Elmwood Park, Illinois

Harold Freiter
Vice Principal
Lord Selkirk Regional
  Comprehensive Secondary
  School
Selkirk, Manitoba, Canada

Leah Gauthier
Director for Curriculum
  and Instruction
Elmwood Park Community
  Unit School District 401
Elmwood Park, Illinois

Kim Gill
Principal
Westwood Elementary School
Greenwood, Arkansas

Lori Griffin
Principal
Ballman Elementary School
Fort Smith, Arkansas

Dan Jenkins
Principal
Norwood Middle School
Oliver Springs, Tennessee

Jeffrey Wasem
Principal
Creekside Middle School
Bentonville, Arkansas

Visit **go.SolutionTree.com/leadership** to download the free reproducibles in this book.

TABLE OF CONTENTS

CHAPTER 3

Strategies for Working With Individuals 57

CHAPTER 4

Strategies for Working With Large Groups 79

CHAPTER 5

Strategies for When Nothing Seems to Work 103

ABOUT THE AUTHOR

 **William A. Sommers, PhD**, of Austin, Texas, continues to be a learner, teacher, principal, author, leadership coach, and consultant. Bill has come out of retirement multiple times to put theory into practice as a principal in high schools and middle schools. He has worked at inner-city schools as well as in high-socioeconomic-status suburban districts. Bill has been a consultant for cognitive coaching, adaptive schools, brain research, poverty, habits of mind, conflict management, and classroom management strategies and is a Marshall Goldsmith certified Stakeholder Centered Coach.

Bill served on the board of trustees of the National Staff Development Council (now Learning Forward) for five years and as president for one year. He is the former Executive Director for Secondary Curriculum and Professional Learning for Minneapolis Public Schools and a school administrator of over thirty-five years. He has also been a Senior Fellow for the Urban Leadership Academy at the University of Minnesota. Bill has served as an adjunct faculty member at Texas State University, Hamline University, University of St. Thomas, St. Mary's University, Union Institute, and Capella University. In addition, he has been a program director for an adolescent chemical dependency treatment center and on the board of a halfway house for twenty years.

Bill has coauthored ten books, *Living on a Tightrope: A Survival Handbook for Principals, Being a Successful Principal: Riding the Wave of Change Without Drowning, Reflective Practice to Improve Schools, A Trainer's Companion, Energizing Staff Development Using Film Clips, Leading Professional Learning Communities, Guiding Professional Learning Communities, The Principal's Field Manual, A Trainer's Companion: Stories to Stimulate Reflection, Conversation, Action,* and *Nine Professional Conversations to Change Our Schools.* Bill has also coauthored chapters in several other books.

To learn more about Bill's work, visit www.learningomnivores.com or follow him @BillSommers8 on Twitter.

To book William A. Sommers for professional development, contact pd@SolutionTree.com.

PREFACE

Story of the Buffalo

The Buffalo on the prairie knows
That when he sees a thunderstorm coming
If he turns and walks away from it
It will last for a long time.
The Buffalo also knows
That if he turns and walks toward the thunderstorm
It will pass more quickly.

—*Suzanne Bailey*

INTRODUCTION
What's the Real Problem?

Almost all conflict is a result
of violated expectations.

—*Blaine Lee*

In my forty years in education, one area continues to expand: conflict. Conflict can be one of the biggest energy sappers and time wasters in classrooms, schools, and districts. Those who have spent time in schools and districts know this is true. A parent demands a principal's attention to a relatively unimportant issue when the principal is trying to get to a teacher observation. Cliques develop in a classroom, and the teacher needs help healing the divisions. Experienced teachers grow wary of new staff members who try to shake things up. A teacher feels ostracized by his collaborative team. The superintendent hands down bad news from the district, leaving the principal to work out the details and assuage her staff's concerns. More time and energy spent on conflict and resistance mean less time and energy spent on learning. Educators go home physically and emotionally drained by the end of the day. The competing commitments of focusing on learning and responding to interpersonal issues erode the available time and energy.

Many of us who work in schools are experiencing a great deal of change. I often hear, "I thought I had problems years ago, but they were nothing compared to today." For instance, new initiatives in social-emotional learning, ever-changing standards, increasing diversity, numbers of students coming to schools from challenging backgrounds, and so on force educators to keep adapting to social and governmental changes. While change can generate excitement and creativity, it can also cause conflict and an uncomfortable, uneasy feeling. As the epigraph quote from Blaine Lee suggests, when people do not get what they think they should or the world does not operate the way they think it could, conflict happens. To glean the positive effects of change, there must be an ongoing foundation of learning.

When I teach leadership to prospective school administrators, my first question is, "How do you feel about dealing with conflict?" Some squirm, some are puzzled, and some are just plain shocked—they came thinking they would sit in a boring class and talk about leadership theories. Then I say, "You don't have to like conflict, but if you really don't want to deal with it, I suggest you leave this class and find another line of work." Leadership is never conflict free. If you are going to work with people, it is going to be messy. That goes for life inside and outside of schools.

Although conflict is inevitable, leaders can still take steps to respond to it positively and effectively. My hope is that this resource can help manage resistance and reduce the stresses of being a leader. If you are looking for a book on the theory of conflict, I can recommend many sources, but this is *not* it. What this book does contain is thirty strategies that I have accumulated over my career as a principal and in central office positions. The strategies in this book are grounded in theory, and I cite this supportive literature. The real use of this book is putting strategies into action. I wrote this book for building and district leaders who are constantly working with people who have competing priorities for schools and students. Leaders might also share these processes with classroom teachers to help them manage conflict with students, parents, and yes, colleagues.

I believe if you want to be an effective leader, you must be able to solve, reframe, and manage conflict and resistance in schools. You cannot control what happens to you; you only have control over how you respond to what happens to you. As Aldous Huxley (1933) said, "Experience is not what happens to a man, it is what a man does with what happens to him" (p. 5). If you cannot manage the conflict, you will never spend enough time on learning. Unresolved conflict will divert intention and attention, usurping time and energy that should be spent on learning for staff and students. This book aims to reduce the time and energy spent on conflict and management issues in order to devote more time to learning. You could find all of these response strategies on your own in disparate resources. However, since time is one of the most important issues for teachers and leaders in schools, the purpose of this book is to save you time.

As a foundation for the conflict-response strategies, the following sections discuss important background information: emotional agility, causes of conflict, and the dangers of ignoring conflict.

Emotional Agility

It is no surprise that one's first reaction to conflict is often an emotional one. Robert Cooper and Ayman Sawaf (1996) write, "The limbic system works approximately 80,000 times faster than the conscious cerebral cortex" (p. 88). Because information reaches the amygdala—the emotional center of the brain and part of the limbic system—thousands of times faster than it reaches the frontal lobe—where rational decisions are made—we will always react emotionally first. I smile when I hear parents or staff say, "This kid is always so emotional." Well, of course! That is what the brain is designed to do. The amygdala and the emotional alarm system keep us out of danger most of the time; long ago, it prevented us from being eaten by lions, tigers, and bears. This, by the way, is why bullying is so devastating to learning in schools and social groups—the bully's aggression triggers the victim's (and often onlookers') emotional threat response, while the rational thought processes needed for learning are shunted aside (Bates, 2015). Additional information on bullying can be found through the Conflict Resolution Education Network (www.creducation.net).

Judith Glaser (2014) writes about the behaviors demonstrated when your brain reacts emotionally to stress or a sense of danger: fight, flight, freeze, or appease. Think about it: when you are attacked verbally or emotionally, don't you want to run or fight back? Fighting can increase the emotional cost. Typically, we have to choose whether to speak truth to power and fight back. Fighting back against someone who is aggressive or skilled in argument can be a waste of time and emotionally draining. Keep in mind that the classical definition of the fight response includes physical attacks, though one hopes these would be rare in school environments.

Flight can be the best response, especially in cases where you feel physically threatened or you have had the same conversation several times. However, in a leadership position, you may not be able to simply walk away. Limit time in situations that sap your emotional energy, and consider whether the best use of all parties' time is to take a break and perhaps continue the conversation later.

Sometimes you may be shocked, and you freeze up. Freezing can be very difficult for you and the person you are in conflict with. You are stressed, unsure of what to do, and perhaps seemingly unable to respond effectively. Your lack of response might frustrate the other person; he or she might even think you are ignoring the problem. We are much better off taking some action if possible.

If you get beyond the initial emotional surge, you might try to appease. Appeasement sometimes can work under the right circumstances, but appeasing involves making a short-term decision without understanding the long-term consequences, which creates further difficulty. Appeasement usually involves making an exception to the rules, and selective enforcement of rules will be harmful to the organization. Yes, there are special circumstances in which you deviate from rules and procedures with good reason. If deviation becomes the norm, however, you will suffer from system dysfunction.

The problem with fight, flight, freeze, and appease is that they are instinctual, emotional reactions, not reasoned responses. As Jennifer Abrams (2019) suggests, the ability to "respond, not react" (p. 57) is critical in developing classrooms, schools, and districts focused on learning. To create new ways of thinking when confronted by conflict and resistance, we need emotional agility (David, 2016). You cannot stop all problems; your only option is to have multiple ways of responding to problems. The time between getting resistance and your own response is the time to create options rather than fight, flight, freeze, or appease. Having a repertoire of responses builds competence and confidence. Professionals who have the repertoire to proactively address conflict will show improved results. These leaders know the best strategies for responding to difficult, emotional situations and have the flexibility to use those strategies in real time (David, 2016). Hence, the purpose of this book is to expand your repertoire of response strategies. Leaders will need a range of responses and the emotional agility—the presence of mind to sidestep unhelpful instinctual reactions—to use those strategies, thereby making them better leaders and models for students, colleagues, and community. The ability to move forward, even in stressful situations, demonstrates exemplary leadership.

Emotional agility will only gain importance as the world continues to evolve and increase in volatility, uncertainty, complexity, and ambiguity (VUCA; Johansen, 2007). Who thinks there will be less conflict in schools in the future? I don't. The question becomes, Will leaders have the repertoire to respond effectively to conflict?

The old ways won't always work—as Marshall Goldsmith (2007) alludes to in the title of his book *What Got You Here Won't Get You There*. Leaders must respond to unpredictability with a different VUCA: vision, understanding, clarity, and agility. Having strategies to manage conflict increases agility in the fast-paced world of schools. Gaining clarity on the issues is foundational in listening, understanding diverse points of view, and determining the preferred future for stakeholders. Agility in dealing with a multitude of issues will become more important as the future continues to evolve.

Causes of Conflict

I met author and conflict resolution expert Bob Chadwick in the mid-1980s. He helped me reframe conflict from avoidance to proactively managing it. Chadwick (2013) believes that conflict is a result of five main issues.

1. Change
2. Power
3. Scarcity
4. Diversity
5. Civility

Change

Try folding your arms. Now take the arm on top and put it on the bottom. Place the bottom arm on top. Does that feel uncomfortable? Change causes many people to be uncomfortable. You might be uncomfortable when you take a golf lesson, try to speak a foreign language, or find your way to the hotel in a strange city. Change means trying something new and often not being very good at it initially. With the responses to resistance in this book, you may not feel comfortable trying a new strategy at first. But the more you do something, the easier it gets. Practice makes the difference.

Anyone who dislikes change is going to be very unhappy in education. Esteemed researcher Shirley Hord and I came up with the saying, "learning is change and change is learning." Schools developed long ago when a finite body of knowledge was important, following rules for the industrial age was imperative for assembly line work, and management by the numbers was the primary leadership strategy. However, we are now and will continue to be in a world of change. So, find ways to deal with change or you will probably be frustrated. Change is not going away. One of my favorite quotes, from author and inspirational speaker Karen Kaiser Clark (1993), is, "Life is change. Growth is optional. Choose wisely." Life will continue to cause change. People will either grow and learn or end up in less control of their lives. Choose wisely by having the necessary resources to manage yourself and your systems daily.

Power

When there is a power differential, conflict can result. People bring their problems to leaders because they think the leader will make a decision in their favor. In this interaction, the leader has power; the parent or staff member or student does not feel like they have power. When people do not get the decision they want, conflict can occur.

People go to those in charge wanting to resolve their conflict by edict. This dynamic is often challenging with larger groups. As a principal, when one or two students come in and express a problem, it is relatively easy to listen and help find positive ways to address the issue. If five, ten, or more students come in to see me, they see me as powerful and want me to order that something be done. The same is true for staff. However, when people do not feel heard, or worse, feel ignored, bigger problems result. If I make a decision without hearing from all parties, the conflict continues. If I listen, clarify the ultimate goal, and lead a discussion about how we might accomplish common goals, the result improves. Trust increases, respect for alternative points of view is honored, and there is less emotional cost.

Remember, conflict has two elements: content and relationships. If you destroy the relationship, the rest will be more difficult. If you can manage the relationship positively, you increase the likelihood of resolving or managing the content of the conflict.

I am constantly reminded to use power wisely, or ego and arrogance can cause trouble. Remember there is power of position and power of the person. People in management roles may have the power of position: there are things they are responsible for and people they are responsible to. True leadership is much more tied to the power of the person: his or her influence, credibility, and caring that allow others to feel comfortable working together toward common goals. Make sure to use power appropriately and for the right reason.

Scarcity

Scarcity always results in conflict. When resources are scarce, people tend to hide and hoard. People worry that there will not be enough for them and that others are getting more than their fair share. This creates an individualist mindset, ripe for conflict. If you want to know how concerned people are about scarcity, walk through the classrooms some evening and check out the closets. You will find boxes of markers, paper, and sometimes even toilet paper. Once, during a budget cut, I knew we could not afford to buy more supplies than we needed. I also knew there were supplies stashed all around the school. I met with the leadership team, and we devised a plan for all teachers to bring their excess supplies to the office so they could be redistributed fairly among the departments. We stayed within our budget, but made sure everyone had what he or she needed.

Parents, businesses, and communities want more from schools than schools were ever designed to provide. As a principal, you are always dealing with at least two areas of scarcity: budgeting and staffing. There is never enough to satisfy every problem and every need, and it is often a zero-sum game. For example, if the English department needs more books and the science department needs more equipment, one wins and one loses. Worse, if you divide the resources evenly, neither group is sufficiently funded, and both are upset. Leaders must address these issues decisively and openly, or conflict will consume a great deal of time and energy.

The worst version of conflict over scarcity is resentment between staff members. I would rather have the staff united against my decision than have a split staff. A team that has or feels it has an "in" crowd (those who get favorable treatment) and an "out" crowd (staff that are viewed as outsiders) will be disruptive and emotionally draining for all. As a principal, sometimes you have to listen to all sides, but then make a call and be accountable for that decision (that is, use your power appropriately). I make sure my colleagues know I want to hear their thoughts on staffing and budgeting, but in the end, it will be my call. That is my role as a principal.

Diversity

People normally think of diversity in terms of race, culture, or ethnicity, and those are real issues that leaders deal with; here, I speak generally about diversity of perspectives. The best learning environments I have seen and been a part of see diversity as a strength, not a problem. In his book *The Wisdom of Crowds*, James Surowiecki (2004) indicates that the teams make better quality decisions than the smartest individual person in the room. My experience confirms that notion that the inclusion of diverse viewpoints results in better decisions that more people support. Without a diversity of beliefs, teams will not make the best of the intellectual horsepower in their people.

Leaders can and should be intentional about including diverse viewpoints. For example, when I am leading a school, I want to develop student leadership. That usually means meeting with the student council. At the end of the first meeting, I ask, "Who is not in the room?" The goal for the next meeting is to find students who are not represented and bring them to the meeting. In this way, we expand influence, get better information from all groups, and build relationships. The diversity of students brings great insight and honors their intelligence and commitment.

When making decisions about the school, do not forget students and parents. They are stakeholders. Including them will reduce the problems created when decisions are made for people instead of with people. Expanding the range of perspectives leads to better decisions.

Along with diverse perspectives, there must be trust among the people in the room. As a principal of a turnaround school, I met with my newly formed leadership team before school started. I began by asking two questions.

1. (Trust) "Looking around, are these the people you want to get into trouble with? We will be working hard and facing many challenges together."

2. (Diverse perspectives) "Will you tell me (the principal) if you think I am wrong? You know the school and community, I don't. You have to be willing to tell me if you think I am leading the team down the wrong path."

Both factors need to be in place for effective collaboration.

Civility

Finally, civility—or lack thereof. Sometimes we do not treat each other very well. Without civility, emotions can spiral out of control. Similar to conflict, in any negotiation or difference of opinion, there are two elements. One is the content, the results of the decision. The other is each party's emotions about the decision and how the decision was made. Emotions can sidetrack any decision and cause conflict. Civility in disagreement means making sure all stakeholders are heard, treating them with respect, and considering their points of view.

Leaders who keep people outside the process, ignore their points of view, and refuse to honor their emotions will put themselves in peril. People who do not feel heard can become less civil because they feel ignored. I try to remember three things H. Stephen Glenn (1988) said in his talk "Developing Capable Young People" at a conference on chemical dependency in St. Cloud, Minnesota. People need to feel like you are listening to them, taking them seriously, and taking a genuine interest in their points of view. I have found this guidance has been a North Star for my leadership over the years.

Having discussed the causes of conflict, I will next review the dangers of ignoring it.

The Dangers of Ignoring Conflict

Addressing conflict is not easy, but it is important. Educators must begin to face unresolved conflict and make organizations physically and emotionally safe while getting the best thinking from their colleagues. As leadership expert Amy Edmondson (2019) writes in her book, *The Fearless Organization*, psychological safety is critical to increasing learning and unleashing creativity to solve problems. Healthy schools and districts have developed relationships and processes to respond to conflicts openly and honestly. Richard Sheridan (2018), cofounder of the software design firm Menlo Innovations, says, "Fear does not make bad news go away. Fear makes bad news go into hiding" (p. 104). If bad news goes into hiding, you will never manage it, deal with it, or get beyond it. Toxic outcomes for the organization and leader will result:

- People withhold information, which limits understanding and reduces the quality of decisions.
- People will ruminate on an issue; negative feelings will fester.
- People will become isolated or form cliques, only sharing with people they think are safe.

In many ways, schools and organizations operate like families. In my consulting and coaching, I have often heard, "We are a family here." That is truer than people realize. Schools, like families, have unspoken rules and rituals. Children take verbal and nonverbal cues from siblings and parents, as students do from staff and staff do from leaders. In *Why Marriages Succeed or Fail,* John Gottman (2012), psychological researcher, author, and professor at the University of Washington, presents a progressive model of marriage that can apply to schools. One major indicator Gottman looks for in families is how people manage conflict. From my experience, this will usually predict the depth of problems in an organization as well. The following sections define the four stages Gottman identifies when resistance and conflict are ignored or ineffectively managed.

Stage 1: Criticism

In the first stage, there is criticism of what someone does and the way he or she does it. Criticism can be productive if people can express their concerns honestly without fear of being ridiculed, state their beliefs and cognitive and affective reasons, and be clear about the goals they want for themselves and students. Left unaddressed, the tendency is to find like-minded people, hang out with those who share their beliefs, and reinforce their own viewpoints and solutions. Isolation is usually the first clue something is not right.

Stage 2: Contempt

In addition to criticism, people start making the differences more personal. Not only do they believe something different, but they also attribute these differences to personal characteristics and intentionally oppose any other beliefs. Left unchallenged, the systemic relationships continue to deteriorate. In addition to having differences of opinion, people see others as being negative. Isolation continues, negative comments and behind-the-back alliances grow, and communication diminishes.

Stage 3: Defensiveness

People start digging in and defending their positions rather than listening to alternative points of view and asking questions to understand. This reduces understanding between differing points of view on real concerns. People reduce their social networks even further and become even more defensive, which drives more people away. The group becomes smaller and more isolated. The goal is to defend positions and diminish options rather than expand solutions to complicated problems. The goal is now to win at all costs rather than to look for ways to get the positives from diverse points of view.

Stage 4: Separation

At this stage, people rarely interact except in formal ways (at all-school meetings and the like). Teachers retreat to their classrooms, sometimes leaving the hallways and cafeterias to the students and a few administrators. The school is not good for learning, building relationships, or improving social-emotional health. Students can feel the divisions among the staff, and administrators have to focus on negative staff feelings, distracting from their learning-centered work. The school continues to fragment, and the sense of community is destroyed.

Luckily, leaders can prevent these stages of relationship deterioration through positive responses to conflict, such as the strategies in this book. It is hard work for courageous people, but your teachers and students are worth it. So, find ways to build relationships, manage conflicts, and create the best environment for students, staff, and community. The next section gives an overview of the contents of each chapter in this book.

How This Book Is Organized

Chapter 1 provides foundational skills that leaders can apply to most conflict situations. Clarifying issues and defining the problem are extremely important when dealing with conflict, resistance, and differences of opinion.

In leadership positions, much of one's time is spent building strong teams that can work together to solve problems. Chapter 2 focuses on working with small groups and bringing people together when conflict might exist. Effective collaboration is key in solving organizational problems. Leaders need all the knowledge and energy they can find in their schools and districts to respond to important issues.

Chapter 3 addresses individuals and how their personal and professional issues affect their performance. This becomes a major task for leaders. The leader must be able to mediate problems and manage differences between educators. When individual professionals feel excluded, feel dismissed, or are in conflict with colleagues, those issues usually end up in the leader's office. Even if they do not actively bring their issues to the principal, the resulting relationship and culture problems in the school will demand the leader's response. Hence, skills in working with individuals become a high priority.

Leaders find themselves in front of large groups on a regular basis. Whether it is school staff, school community meetings, or presentations to district committees and boards, conflict can emerge in these settings. Chapter 4 offers ways to manage large groups.

Finally, chapter 5 presents some ideas for when nothing seems to be working. When you have tried a number of strategies to address an individual or group conflict without success, these approaches can help address more persistent problems.

Even though the chapters categorize the strategies according to their primary use with teams, individuals, and large groups, you will find you can use these strategies in multiple situations. Sometimes you might use an individual strategy with teams or vice versa. Throughout the chapters, you will find vignettes inspired by real events that illustrate the types of conflicts to which the response strategies might apply.

Administrators have used the strategies in this book successfully for many years. The stories are from real experiences in schools, districts, and communities. All of these strategies have worked and can work. But the truth is, all of these strategies *won't* work. That is the reality—nothing works all the time or in every situation. There are no silver bullets. A friend and colleague of mine, Michael Ayers, former 3M leadership trainer and parent in one of the schools where I was principal, asked me in 2004, "Why do you have twenty-five ways to solve conflict?" My response, as a veteran school administrator, was, "I had twenty-four, and none of them worked." Leaders must be willing to try new approaches and constantly expand their repertoires. As you can tell from this book, I continue to expand my own repertoire.

When trying new strategies, be sure to stick with them long enough to truly discover if they work. Educators often jump around too quickly, before they can get good at each strategy. Eric Abrahamson (2004), professor of management at Columbia University, in his book *Change Without Pain*, said educators are afflicted with "repetitive change syndrome." We keep jumping from idea to idea without finding out what works. In his book *The Dip*, Seth Godin (2007), author, blogger, and entrepreneur, explains that when we try something new, it often does not show immediate positive results because we have not really integrated the new process or program, so we bail and look for something new. One additional requirement, from Simon Sinek's (2009) book *Start With Why*, is to define clear reasons for change, rather than changing for the sake of changing. When people do not know why they are changing, they continually move on to the next new idea, which reduces the chance of ever fully implementing the prior ideas or collecting enough specific data on their effectiveness. To counteract this lack of focus and the speed of changing programs and processes, I am suggesting leaders have a wide repertoire of strategies to respond to the immediate issues that arise, manage conflicts that have been unresolved in the organization, and find out under what conditions a new approach works and for which students and staff.

Educators need to proactively manage conflict to spend less time and energy on nonproductive issues. You want to spend your time wisely and productively on positive outcomes, not immersed in conflict. Proactive responses to conflict prevent escalation and accelerate learning in organizations. To begin our learning together, I want to start with a few foundational skills that you can use in most situations. Knowing these skills will make it easier to navigate the remaining strategies.

CHAPTER 1
Foundational Skills

A problem well-stated is half-solved.

—Charles Kettering

To begin building a repertoire of strategies to respond to resistance, this chapter focuses on four prerequisite skills: (1) clarifying issues; (2) verbalizing specific problems; (3) admitting when you are wrong; and (4) admitting when you don't know something. This chapter explores the following four strategies to address each of the aforementioned skills, which will prepare you for success. Each one is a specific linguistic skill that will help clarify issues and identify the real problems. These skills will help you be more effective with the other responses to resistance in this book.

Response Strategy 1: Use Linguistic Skills to Increase Specificity

Response Strategy 2: Paraphrase

Response Strategy 3: Accept Responsibility

Response Strategy 4: Say "I Don't Know"

RESPONSE STRATEGY 1
Use Linguistic Skills to Increase Specificity

One afternoon at about 5:30 p.m., I got a call from a parent.

Parent: Your school sucks.

Me: The whole school?

Parent: No, it's the math department.

Me: The whole math department?

Parent: No, it is Mr. Lindquist.

Me: What did Mr. Lindquist say or do that makes you say he is not good?

Parent: My son got an F on the last geometry test.

Me: Will you bring your son into my office in the morning so we can address this problem?

Steve Lindquist was a great teacher, and I trusted him. Obviously, the student had gone home, complained to the parent about a poor grade, and blamed the teacher and school for not teaching him geometry. Notice that the conflict began with a very broad statement—the whole school sucking. What am I supposed to do with that? Have a staff meeting and tell them to quit sucking? By digging deeper, we were able to define a much more specific issue that got at the heart of the problem—the failed geometry test. The parent, the son, Steve, and I met in the morning. Steve took the student to his office, and they developed a plan so the student could get better at geometry.

· · · · · ·

This story points out the importance of defining what the problem is before jumping to a solution. If you can't define the issue, you can't solve it. This is equally true for leaders, teachers, and even students. Imagine a student who is beginning a science fair project or a research paper. Before even designing the project, they must be able to answer questions like, What is the problem or question you are trying to solve or answer? In the final analysis, what are you trying to find out? Without a pinpoint question to investigate, they will never be able to find an answer or solution. Similarly, in trying to make a difference for everyone, lots of demands and lots of ideas often divert teachers. Unfortunately, without focus and implementation, educators do not stay with a program or process. More incoming demands intercept intentions and attention. This reminds me of a Russian proverb: "If you chase two rabbits, you will not catch either one" (Keller, 2013, p. i). Responding to conflict requires a clear definition of the problem and a focus on chasing down the solution.

Whether the conflict involves a student, staff member, or community member, if a leader cannot figure out what the real issue is, he or she will never be able to solve it. Too many times, the initial problem is not the real issue. As in the previous vignette, "the whole school sucks" does not express the real issue nor identify any pathway for managing or resolving the problem. When an issue is undefined, time is wasted, frustration grows on both sides, and the resistance gets more entrenched. However, you have to start where the other person or group is and work to gain specificity. To that end, one can begin clarifying the problem by identifying fuzzy language.

Fuzzy language usually means fuzzy thinking. There are five common types of fuzzy language (Laborde, 1987).

1. Unspecified nouns
2. Unspecified verbs
3. Rules
4. Generalizations
5. Comparators

Figure 1.1 (page 20) describes each of these types and shows how you can use the fingers on your hand as a memory hook. The following sections provide more detail.

Unspecified Nouns

Unspecified nouns make assumptions and promote stereotypes for groups of people, places, and things: The students won't come on time. The teachers don't care about the kids. The administrators are not supporting the teachers. The response: *Which* students are not

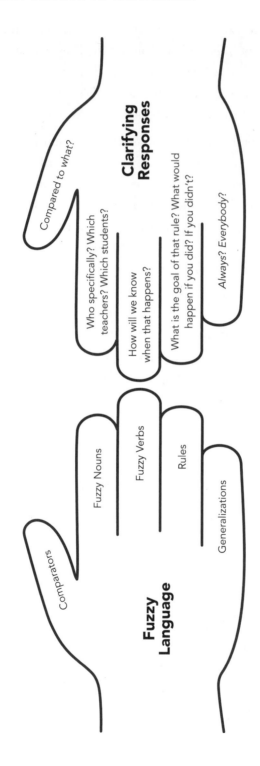

Source: Adapted from Laborde, 1987.

Figure 1.1: Responding to fuzzy language.

coming on time? *Which* teachers do you think don't care about kids? *Which* administrators are not supporting the teachers? I have never found that all the students, all the teachers, or all the administrators are doing or not doing something. Without finding out who, how many, and what they are doing or not doing, you will never solve the issue. Making changes for everybody because of a few is overkill and reduces the commitment of the most supportive because they receive blame along with everyone else.

Unspecified Verbs

When confronted with unspecified verbs, clarify actions. In the example of administrators purportedly failing to support teachers, one might ask, "What are you hearing or seeing that makes you think administrators are not supporting the teachers?" Getting specific about the behaviors provides the necessary information to confront the issue and change behavior if needed. Another example is when I hear a teacher say, "I want the students to know the times table." My response is, "What will the students be doing or saying when they know the times table?" Does the teacher want them to be able to fill out a ten-by-ten multiplication table? Answer 70 percent of the odd-numbered problems assigned? Give me specifics, and we will be able to tell whether we are successful.

Rules

Rules are universal statements that people make about their behavior. They might be positive or negative, and often involve terms like *can't, could never,* and *should always*. You will hear comments like these:

- "I could never teach a creative lesson."
- "I should only teach content."
- "I will never like Billy."

When rule-based thinking is apparent from the language used, it gives insights into what is behind those statements. Once the person or group voices their assumptions explicitly, they are better able to choose a response and thereby possibly modify their thinking and behavior.

Leaders can draw attention to rule-based thinking by asking things like, "What would happen if [you broke that rule]?" or "Who made the rule that you [can or can't do that]?" Some possible responses to the preceding examples are as follows.

- "What would happen if you did teach a creativity process?"
- "How might you include relationships with your content?"
- "Who made the rule that you will never like Billy?"

Real or perceived rules can restrict thinking and limit the possibilities of successful learning, teaching, and collaboration. People do need boundaries for behavior. They also need to challenge rules when they get in the way of learning.

Generalizations

When my daughter was in middle school, she came home the first week of school, and I asked, "How was school?" She said she liked middle school but needed a few things. I, being the supportive dad and seeking to clarify unspecified nouns, asked, "What things?" She said, "I need a pair of Guess jeans." I countered, "Why do you need them?" She responded, "Everybody has them."

Since I teach this language problem of universal quantifiers, I was confident in my ability to handle this. I said, "Everybody?" using the proper skeptical intonation. She said, "Yes, everybody." Drat, I had thought that would do it. I responded, "Everybody at Valley View Middle School has Guess jeans?" She said with a little more gusto, "Yes, everybody." I still thought I was in control and said, "Do you know anyone at VVMS who does not have Guess jeans?" She responded indignantly, "You know what I mean." I said, "Yes, and I want you to know that I know what you mean."

Having at least drawn her attention to the problem of universal qualifiers, I asked, "How much do they cost?" She said, "$65.00." Now, keep in mind that at this time, a typical pair of jeans cost $10.00. When I recovered from the shock, I said, "Here is $20.00, and you can work for the rest." She said, "I need them now." I replied, "My contract with you is to cover your rear end, not decorate it." She turned in a huff and went to her mom, who gave her the rest of the money. Of course, then I was in conflict with my spouse. You can't win them all.

. . . . . .

Generalizations, or universal quantifiers, are similar to unspecified nouns but even broader. They include words like *everyone*, *nobody*, *everything*, *nothing*, and so on. You will hear comments such as the following.

- "Everybody is going."
- "Nobody does their share."
- "You never let me do anything."

These statements make you believe the problem is everything, everybody, and will never change. Here are three options to confront and clarify these generalizations.

1. **Intonation:** "*Everybody?*" The voice goes up at the end. The answer is usually, "No, not everybody."

2. **Exaggeration:** "*Not even one single, individual person* in this school does their share of the work?" Make it bigger than what is meant. Usually you hear back, "Well, no, a few are doing their share."

3. **Exception:** "Can you think of anything I *have* let you do?" This forces the person to identify exceptions to his or her own rule, thereby clarifying the thinking. The response most of the time is, "OK, there are *some* things."

And, when none of this works? My answer might be a top-down supervisor's decision. Sometimes people might be very stubborn in their refusal to accept your decisions or leadership. I do not like to say, "Because I said so," but when the safety of people or ethical behavior is involved, leaders must have that option to assert their supervisory role. I do not take this lightly and do not use this very often—if "because I said so" is the norm, there are deep culture issues to address—but sometimes it is necessary. I will say that is if it is absolutely a requirement for a physically and emotionally safe environment. For example, "There will be no drugs or alcohol in this school."

Comparators

The final category of fuzzy language is comparators. This kind of language makes assumptions about quality and value, using words like *best* and *worst* with no outside standard. Advertisers frequently use this language cue, which may be why it seems so natural to people. People commonly use words like *better*, *best*, *worst*, and *least* in isolation, without any other option or objective standard to compare it to. The car company Toyota once used the slogan "The best built cars in the world." This vague superlative even led the Advertising Standards Authority for Ireland to rule that Toyota must stop using the claim in advertisements because it could not be proven (Pope, 2016). Other examples of comparators include the following.

- **"We use best practices."** Compared to what other practices? Who decided this was the best one?
- **"This is the worst idea I have ever heard."** Compared to what other ideas? How is it worse?

Leaders should probe to find out what other options have been considered rather than accepting that something is the best or worst.

With these foundational language skills to clarify the issue at hand, further strategies to respond to and solve the conflict become more useable and effective. Remember, if you cannot define the problem, you will be unable to manage the issue or you will waste a lot of time without making progress.

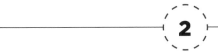

RESPONSE STRATEGY 2

Paraphrase

Listening is a key aspect of creating a relationship. When someone feels that you are not listening, he or she will likely get agitated and become less willing to listen to you, and thus the chance of resolution diminishes. One way to communicate that you are listening to someone is to paraphrase what he or she has said. Paraphrasing is saying the big idea, main points, and maybe a few of the speaker's reasons in your own words. Paraphrasing sends two messages to the other person.

1. I have listened to you.
2. I am checking for accuracy to ensure I have understood you correctly.

When you paraphrase, it should be shorter than what the speaker originally said; it is a summary. If a paraphraser babbles on and on, he or she will talk around the problem and potentially dominate the conversation instead of listening. Another key feature to emphasize in paraphrasing is that you must use your own words rather than parroting exactly what the speaker said. Repeating the speaker's words exactly often comes across as just going through the motions, rather than a genuine attempt to understand.

The goal of paraphrasing is to make sure the speaker knows you have the big idea, have listened to his or her concerns, and understand the problem. This can be very affirming to the speaker, especially in emotionally charged situations. As Arthur L. Costa and Robert J. Garmston (2002) write, paraphrasing can also improve communication by increasing clarity. Paraphrasing is a check by the receiver that they understand what the speaker is saying. This saves time and helps focus the conversation on the real issues.

After paraphrasing, you can go one step further and give the speaker a chance to correct your paraphrase or add to what you said. Questions such as "Is there anything I missed?" or "Do I understand the situation?" provide that opportunity and an important check for clarity and accuracy.

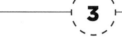

RESPONSE STRATEGY 3
Accept Responsibility

At some point, most people have gotten into conflicts and subsequently realized that a misunderstanding was their fault, or the conflict stemmed from their own mistake. The best (and perhaps only) thing to do in this situation is to acknowledge the error and accept responsibility. If you are wrong, stop and admit it. An apology is the quickest way for the other party to know you have heard their complaint, you understand, and you are committed to correcting the issue. If you are wrong and you admit it, you will build trust. Do not try to cover up problems. It is your responsibility to confirm the other person's resistance is warranted—the problem is real and a result of your error. Covering it up will destroy your credibility, which will limit your influence and others' confidence in your leadership. When leaders take responsibility for their mistakes, they model that behavior for staff and foster a safe environment for others to acknowledge their own errors. Be fully responsible if it is your fault. Sometimes, as a leader, you share the responsibility for others' mistakes as well. Perhaps you made assumptions or gave unclear directions. Be sure to acknowledge your responsibility in these situations too.

Sam Horn (1996; see also Horn, 2012) described a three-part process for taking responsibility if you are wrong: "Agree, Apologize, Act" (p. 27).

- Agree with the person or people who bring the problem to your attention.
- Apologize for making the error.
- Take action to repair, take corrective action, or take steps to make it right.

As an example, early in my career, a student missed too many days to receive credit in a class. The school counselor found the student and brought him to me. As I conferenced with the student and the counselor, I found out the student was experiencing homelessness—living in a car, trying to maintain basic hygiene in school bathrooms, and not always able to find transportation to school. I agreed that our attendance policy did not foresee a student being homeless, apologized for making the assumption he didn't care about school, and took action by creating an independent study contract for one of his required classes. I learned a great deal from this experience and created a better relationship with the student. From this solution, the student was able to stay on track to graduate.

Taking responsibility for your actions helps build and reinforce trust. Denial, diversion, or distorting information will ultimately diminish trust, complicating your future interactions with the other party.

RESPONSE STRATEGY 4

Say "I Don't Know"

In leadership, there are two phrases you need to master: *I'm sorry* and *I don't know*. Be able to say these two with total authenticity and mean it. The previous strategy discussed the importance of apologizing and taking responsibility. Saying "I don't know" when you don't know is just as crucial. For one thing, if you try to pretend that you have all the answers, you will quickly be found out. Having the sense to admit you don't know will increase trust. Being vulnerable shows you are a learner and have a mature sense of your strengths and limitations.

Beyond simply admitting that you do not know something, it is important to provide a path forward. Give what information you do have or assure the person that you will look into it. If someone asks you a question to which you do not know the answer, you can respond as follows.

- "What I do know about it is . . ."
- "I'll find out and get back to you."
- "This didn't work out the way I expected. Let's devise a better solution together."

Say "I don't know" if you really don't know. Nothing causes a decrease in trust faster than trying to fake it. It is as simple as that.

Summary

This chapter covered four foundational strategies for responding to resistance: clarifying issues with specific language, paraphrasing to help get issues on the table, admitting when you are wrong, and admitting when you do not know something. All of these strategies will help build trust and open the conversation between the leader and other parties to the conflict. You can use these communication tactics in combination with the strategies in upcoming chapters to make interactions proceed more smoothly.

As we review this chapter, your authenticity is determined by your honesty. Saying when you don't know and accepting responsibility will help establish your authenticity. Acting consistently will foster your staff's trust in you as a leader. Furthermore, using the linguistic skills of paraphrasing and specificity tells your colleagues you will not waste their time. You are willing to get to the heart of overt and covert issues. Specificity skills will assist you in uncovering core problems and spending less time on the surface problems. Learning and applying the skills from this chapter will be valuable in making the remaining strategies more effective. The next chapter covers strategies for working with teams.

CHAPTER 2

Strategies for Working With Teams

Teaming in today's and tomorrow's world
will be about learning. Teaming and learning
are here to stay. Enjoy learning about it.

—Edgar H. Schein

With the foundation of the skills in chapter 1, the following strategies will be easier to use. While most of the responses in this book can be used with individuals, small groups, and large groups, I start with small groups because a majority of school leaders' work will be done in smaller groups—grade-level teams, departments, leadership teams, and so on. Professional learning communities (PLCs) are a major organizer for schools, and directly focus on teamwork for student and staff learning. By nature, some of these team meetings will involve smart people who may not agree.

This chapter provides the following strategies that can be helpful when working with teams.

Response Strategy 5: Make It a Successful Marriage

Response Strategy 6: Shift From Conflict to Consensus

Response Strategy 7: Unify Different Work Styles

Response Strategy 8: Develop Team Players

Response Strategy 9: Use *Team* as a Verb

Response Strategy 10: Identify Sharks, Carps, and Dolphins

Response Strategy 11: Differentiate Cognitive and Affective Conflicts

Response Strategy 12: Name the Elephants in the Room

RESPONSE STRATEGY 5

Make It a Successful Marriage

A five-person middle school team was operating with two new members after two teachers had moved out of the district over the summer. In October, one of the original members came to see me. She said the team was not working well together, a significant change from the year before. Several other staff members were starting to comment about the team's dysfunction. Even parents were noticing a change in the team's unity.

After observing several team meetings in November, I realized they were a group but not a team. They were not committed to each other and lacked common goals. We held an offsite meeting to determine whether the team could improve and work together. After giving each member a chance to express his or her opinion of what the issues were with the team, I displayed a chart of Gottman's (2012) four stages of a failing marriage: (1) criticism, (2) contempt, (3) defensiveness, and (4) separation.

I asked the team members to indicate where they would place themselves on the four stages and why. One was at contempt, three were at defensiveness, and one was at separation. Then, I asked what each member would need in order to start trusting and building this team. This is an important shift—at some point, the conversation must move from what you do not want to what you do want. If you cannot establish a vision and goals, you really cannot create a pathway to get there.

We did get some agreements that day on how each member would contribute to the team. We followed up each week of the spring semester to assess the agreements and commitments to working differently. The team did make progress by working together more effectively. Communication between staff members increased and there was a reduction in anger, resentment, and judgments. The follow-up at weekly meetings was imperative to address issues quickly and objectively. At the end of that year, one team member left teaching, and another moved to another state. Another new team was formed, but this time we spent time proactively developing the new team during the summer before the school year started. Developing relationships within the team is an important step, especially before the pressure and stress of the daily work with students.

· · · · · ·

The introduction (page 12) presented Gottman's (2012) four stages of unaddressed conflict. This strategy applies those concepts to make positive changes in our work as leaders. Leaders must step into conflicts to protect relationships and school culture. To stop the possibility of a downward spiral, the leader must neutralize the negative and start building positive outcomes.

First, the leader must be able to identify the four stages when they present themselves in team interactions. Table 2.1 (page 34) displays questions and statements that you might hear from colleagues when working relationships have begun to deteriorate. In addition to listening for statements and attitudes like those shown in table 2.1, a leader can also ask the members of a dysfunctional team to self-identify the stage that they are in, as exemplified in the previous vignette.

Once you have identified the stage of deterioration, you can work on helping the team to rebuild their relationships. To help set a

Table 2.1: Identifying Deteriorating Relationships

STAGE	SAMPLE STATEMENTS
Criticism	• Whose fault is this? • I was hurt by your actions, but I didn't tell you. • How is what you believe about learning similar and different from your teammates? • What needs to happen for this team to be efficient and effective? • Do you let things build up rather than dealing with issues in a timely manner? • My emotions got the best of me instead of being specific about the actions.
Contempt	• I believe their faults are part of their personality. • I put the person down rather than identify the issues. It becomes personal. • I start thinking of ways to get even. • I won't give any credit to other people since I don't respect them.
Defensiveness	• We hear a lot of "Yes, but . . ." in our meetings. • People do not take responsibility for their actions or part in the problem. • We hear a lot of whining. • There are many excuses rather than accountability.
Separation	• I would rather stay quiet than state my truth. • Molehills become mountains. • I never hear anything positive. It is always complaining. • I had to calm down, so I left.

positive tone and build a positive relationship among team members, the following are actions the leader can take.

- **Show interest:** It is better to be interested than interesting. Being interested focuses on the other person; being interesting focuses on you. Ask questions rather than make statements. Listen to others' points of view. Are there things you agree with? What are your concerns? Be curious about what a team member thinks or how a team member might engage students.

- **Show you care:** Demonstrate that you care about the other person and their point of view. Ask team members to express their states of mind at the beginning of the meeting. Sometimes outside problems exist that divert attention. Establishing personal contexts creates an understanding, empathetic environment.

- **Be appreciative:** Nobody is all good or all bad. Look for ways to affirm others' contributions to the larger mission. Affirm any positive intentions and actions. Some schools have informal awards that allow staff to recognize a colleague for what he or she did for colleagues or students. The person who receives the recognition chooses the next recipient. Give gratitude to group members about what they have done for students or staff since the last meeting.

- **Be empathetic:** Conversations usually have content and underlying emotions. Pay attention to the emotions—they drive lots of decisions. Find the underlying values and goals of the person. What we think can divide us; what we feel can unite us. Everyone knows what anger, sadness, gladness, fear, and rejection feel like—state emotions publicly.

- **Increase your rate of positive comments:** Negative comments have more impact than positive ones.

Gottman's (2012) research shows there needs to be a ratio of five positive comments for every one negative comment. Barbara Fredrickson (2009), in her book *Positivity*, recommends a three-to-one ratio. In either case, emphasizing positive communication moves relationships forward. Making positive comments to coworkers can help avert a cycle of criticism that begins a downward spiral.

- **Joke around:** The group that can play together increases their chance of staying together. How do you and the school celebrate? What rituals do you have? I strongly recommend improv classes and other opportunities for creativity, communication, and collaboration. Students, school staff, and district personnel can work together better by playing together.

RESPONSE STRATEGY 6

Shift From Conflict to Consensus

A two-member department was in conflict. One member had been in the school for twenty years. The second member was new to the department, having replaced a retiring teacher. Within two months, staff noticed the unhappiness in the department, and anger emerged on both sides. Once aware, the leader tried to resolve the conflict, and met with both teachers. After listening to both people state the issues in their own words, as well as their feelings, the leader helped the two teachers agree on how they would treat each other with clearly defined job responsibilities. The principal set a monthly meeting to monitor how well the teachers were honoring the agreements.

The working relationship was still fragile and not every agreement was being completed, but the monthly meetings with the frank discussions and agreed-on actions reduced the hostility in the department and allowed the teachers to perform their jobs better. However, the situation was still far from ideal, and the principal ended up having a hard conversation with the newer teacher later in the year. The new person put in for another transfer for the following school year and found a much better fit. This goes to show that even with good strategies, not every conflict can be perfectly resolved.

· · · · · ·

Most people react emotionally when they feel attacked. The key is how you fight or stand your ground to work things out. This will take courage to stay in the conversations, humility to accept responsibility for your own part in the conflict, and confidence to stay out of guilt and shame. Here are four specific steps that can help reduce the conflict.

1. **Calm down:** You need to breathe to keep oxygen flowing. Remember your amygdala, the emotional center of your brain, will react emotionally. You want to be in the neocortex where your best thinking occurs. Daniel Murrell (2018) reports when someone feels angry or under attack, the brain produces adrenaline, and it can take one hour for the adrenaline rush to subside to normal levels. During that time, it is important to keep calm and clarify the situation.

2. **Speak nondefensively:** Talk in *I* statements. Starting statements with *you* can make the recipient feel blamed and cause him or her to react emotionally. Focus on wants and goals for the future, rather than on past negative behavior. To be nondefensive in your statements is one of the most powerful ways to get resolution or at least management of the issue. Also, be aware of your body language. If you look aggressive or lean forward, the other person or group may read it as a power move.

3. **Validation:** People want to know they have positive qualities. Validating positive contributions helps defuse

the emotional responses. When facilitating these kinds of conversations, I ask, "What do you like or admire about the other person?" I have had amazing shifts with that question. Each person feels validated; we can get to the goal faster and then create a pathway to get to the goal with specific steps.

4. **Overlearning:** Try and try again. This is not a one-off strategy. Keep trying the first three items in the list, learn from each interchange, and process what you have learned with a critical friend, someone who will be honest giving you real feedback and suggestions.

With this foundation, the leader can facilitate a conversation between the two parties. You will notice in the following example that both teachers get a chance to respond to each of the following questions, and the leader should alternate who answers each question first. This is important because it shows balance; nobody always goes first. The sequence is designed to get the issues out in the open and consider what will happen if the parties fail to resolve or manage the conflict. After that, the process helps the parties identify what they want (the goal), what they will do (actions they will take to make the goal a reality), and how they will know they are getting closer to managing the issue (the assessment plan). Visit **go.SolutionTree.com /leadership** to download a free reproducible version of this process.

- **What are the issues between you two that need to be addressed, and how do you feel about them?** Pose this question to Teacher A. Once Teacher A is finished, ask the same question of Teacher B.

- **What is the worst possible outcome if we cannot solve these issues?** This time, prompt Teacher B to respond to this question first. Then ask the same question to Teacher A. This helps let each one vent their frustrations. Venting is needed so each side feels heard and releases their pent-up frustration.

- **What is the best possible outcome if we can solve these issues?** Ask Teacher A; then, Teacher B answers. This helps define the goal they both want. Thus, there is a point of agreement for moving forward.

- **What strategies and actions are *you* willing to take to make the best possible outcomes a reality?** Direct this question to Teacher B, then Teacher A. This gets you to an action plan and agreements on what actions they are committing to in the future. Both sides can identify what they are willing to do.

- **What will be the evidence that we are making progress toward the best possible outcomes?** Teacher A responds first; when he or she is done speaking, Teacher B answers. This identifies an assessment plan. There can be short-term and long-term results.

- **How often shall we meet to make sure we are living up to our agreements?** Teacher B answers this question, followed by Teacher A. This final prompt is critical. Without follow up, commitments typically are short lived.

While this strategy is designed for responding to conflict between two individual teachers, I have also used this process with whole faculty groups, with athletics and activities groups, and with students individually. Clarifying the issue, what you are going to do about it, and the metrics to know how it is going helps move resolution forward.

RESPONSE STRATEGY 7

Unify Different Work Styles

Individual people have different work styles. It is important to know your staff members' work styles to best manage and collaborate with them. First, find out whether your inner circle—such as assistant principals and administrative staff—works independently or collaboratively. Sometimes if a team is not working together, it is simply because they have different work styles and have not learned to accommodate each other. Imagine a school with three assistant principals: one highly intelligent and lacking human relation skills, another an advocate who focuses on building relationships with students, and a third who is competent about instruction and assessment but a conflict-avoidant person who tends to sit back and not say much in meetings. It is easy to see how these people would find it easier to work independently than to reconcile their different work styles.

Rick Brinkman and Rick Kirschner (2012) present four basic work styles (see figure 2.1).

- **Get it done:** This person is task oriented and wants results, but can be impulsive and too quick to make decisions.
- **Get it right:** This type does not want to be wrong and takes a long time attending to details, but tends to over-plan and prepare.
- **Get along:** This person prioritizes relationships and likes to talk to people; sometimes this gets in the way of getting work done.
- **Get appreciated:** This type works hard for approval and is critical to making organizations run smoothly, but can lose motivation when work goes unrecognized.

Each of these styles has positives. However, when overused, these strengths can become negative.

- Getting it done is a plus, especially in a crisis when fast results are needed. Overused it can cause a person to be abrasive or abusive, not being aware of the emotional side of change.
- Getting it right is important, especially in doing budgets, keeping buses on time, and making sure procedures are

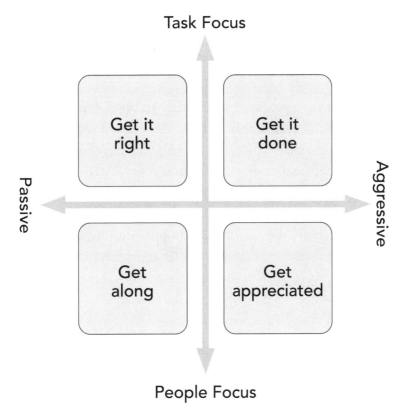

Source: Adapted from Brinkman & Kirschner, 2012.

Figure 2.1: Four basic work styles.

followed. Overused, it can slow everything down so much that people do not believe anything productive will happen. Spending an hour looking for a penny is not helpful.

- Getting along helps the social glue that connects people in organizations. Overused, you spend lots of time hearing each and every opinion while other commitments wait. There needs to be a balance between hearing people out and getting things done in a timely fashion.

- Getting appreciation brings a positive emotional reward to work and encourages continued or increased effort. People need to feel appreciated, especially those doing the work behind the scenes. Recognition cannot be fake or enabling. Overused, seeking appreciation can turn into working only if there will be recognition in the end. Resentment can result when there is no recognition for their efforts.

Many leaders get promoted because they get things done. However, if they steamroll people, they will find themselves isolated. Get-it-right leaders are highly competent, making sure every report is complete and accurate, but they can frustrate people since they take so much time to feel secure in their decisions. The get-along people are the social glue that can help bind teams together. However, wanting to connect and talk can spiral into time-wasting, and time in schools is the most precious resource. Get-appreciated workers seem to always be there when needed and adapt when there is a void in the system; noticing and recognizing hard work are important for the emotional health of the school and district.

Of course, no leader or staff member has all these traits, but they can balance strengths and challenges by creating teams that include a mix of types. For existing teams, leverage the strengths of each person. As a get-it-done kind of leader, I needed assistants that focused on getting it right. To balance my role of confronting personnel problems, I made an effort to use get-along traits. I identified support staff who were get-appreciated types to ensure they felt recognized for their essential work.

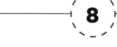

RESPONSE STRATEGY 8

Develop Team Players

Many people claim to be team players, but what does that look like in practice? Business management author Patrick Lencioni (2016) identifies three main factors to being that ideal team player.

1. **Humble:** Humility is the single greatest and most indispensable attribute of being a team player. There are two basic types of people who show a lack of humility—arrogant people and people with low self-confidence. Either of these can have negative effects on their contributions to and the internal relationships within the team.

2. **Hungry:** People who are hungry are self-motivated and diligent. They work hard even without oversight. Assess who is hungry for learning, hungry for positive results, and hungry for working on and in a culture of learning.

3. **Smart:** Smart simply refers to a person's common sense about people. As we all know, there are different kinds of smart. Intellectual horsepower in content areas is important, and social intelligence might be even more powerful when working as a team. The question to ask is: Does the person contribute to the team's intelligence?

Ideal team players "possess adequate measures of humility, hunger, and people smarts. They have little ego when it comes to needing credit for their contributions" (Lencioni, 2016, p. 172). Leaders can use this model in hiring, supervision, development, and evaluation of the effectiveness of a team.

Depending on which attributes a person already has, develop strategies to invite or move each staff member to the middle sweet spot. If a person has none of the three factors, they may not be able to contribute to the school. Consider the following descriptions of those who have only one of the factors and how leaders can develop them.

- **The pawn (humble only):** Humble people tend to sit back, agree with everything, and avoid making waves. Coach them to participate more, find their voice, and increase their professional efficacy.

- **The bulldozer (hungry only):** Hungry people can be very aggressive and abrasive. If they cannot be more humble by listening and honoring other people's point of view, they can be destructive to teamwork, and that may need to be addressed through an individual conversation about how the person's work style affects the team. Provide a chance to talk and provide guidance. If that fails, a formal improvement plan may be necessary.

- **The charmer (smart only):** We certainly need intellectual horsepower in our schools. We can learn a lot from smart people. The caution is that they can be arrogant, thinking they always have the answer. The result is that people tend to stay silent around them, keeping their good ideas to themselves. Leaders need to balance participation. Smart people need to be humble and listen to others to be good contributors.

Some team members might possess two out of the three factors.

- **The accidental mess-maker (humble and hungry):** Humble and hungry people are usually hard workers and do listen to others. Beware that they may not see potential barriers or problems ahead. Guiding them to be more reflective and learn from experience is very important. One way to do this is to ask for a plan of action prior to taking action. This gives the leader a sense of their plans and provides an opportunity for feedback.

- **The lovable slacker (humble and smart):** Humble and smart people are constantly learning and applying. Left alone, they might take the easy way—they are smart and can do the work, but they are not ambitious. These people have great potential but may stay away from challenges since they are not hungry with new ideas. Find them, challenge them, and try to get them in leadership or mentoring roles so they contribute their knowledge, skills, and applications.

- **The skillful politician (hungry and smart):** Staff members who are smart and hungry normally have political savvy as well. They know how to manage the system. Their arrogance can get in the way and keep others from contributing. They seem to demand airtime in meetings because they believe they have the answer. Leaders need to make sure to give others time to put their ideas on the table. They should facilitate meetings in such a way that everyone can participate and all proposals are vetted for purpose, intended results, accuracy, and compatibility with the school goals. Smart and hungry colleagues run the risk of thinking they have the only answer.

Knowing where a staff member fits into this model can help the leader select a strategy to facilitate the best performance. A school or district needs many people with diverse skills. Understanding their strengths and the weaknesses can help direct the leader's efforts to expand the strengths and reduce the challenges.

RESPONSE STRATEGY 9

Use *Team* as a Verb

Teaming is a verb that means continually monitoring and working to keep growing productive teams in a respectful way. High-performing teams feature high humility and low ego. They focus on group intelligence, not the most academic person in the room. They want people who are learners in their own right bringing in diverse ideas to make their projects better. Intellectual horsepower is important, but the affective connection between team members is just as important. To get the best results, teams need both.

We form teams to accomplish many goals. Being on a team does not mean the people are teaming. Without that monitoring and nurturing, a team becomes a group or a mob, which often involves more conflict. Teams that are teaming work to support each other, make sure conversations are clear about their goals, and share the individual repertoire so everyone can excel. In that way, this is a proactive strategy.

Edmondson (2012) identifies four pillars of effective teaming.

1. **Speaking up:** Teaming depends on honest, direct conversation between individuals, including asking questions, seeking feedback, and discussing errors.

2. **Collaboration:** Teaming requires a collaborative mindset and behaviors—both within and outside a given unit of teaming—to drive the process. Team members must share information and feel comfortable seeking help and feedback.

3. **Experimentation:** Teaming involves a tentative approach to action that recognizes the novelty and uncertainty inherent in every interaction between individuals. However, the team must have the freedom to experiment with unproven actions.

4. **Reflection:** Teaming relies on the use of explicit observations, questions, and discussions of processes and outcomes. Talking about mistakes and learning from them should be the norm.

When people can speak openly and honestly, trust increases. They do not have to moderate what they say because team members assume positive intentions. They collaborate by sharing knowledge, skills, and applications around student and staff learning. A great team tries things—they take responsible risks because they want everyone to succeed. Finally, they reflect on what happened. If something did not work, they stop doing it that way. If it works, they add it to the team repertoire to gain flexibility in addressing diverse student needs.

Leaders have a critical role in supporting and facilitating teaming, since better decisions come from the group. Consider the following guidelines.

- Talk openly about learning. Good decisions come from a focus on what we are learning, not fault-finding.

- Make others feel welcome and encouraged. Psychological safety is foundational in aiding teams to express the best ideas and employ processes that make them even better.

- Try new things in new ways to see if there are better ways of teaching and learning. Sheridan (2018) has a quote posted in the Menlo Innovations office: Make Mistakes Fastr (not a typo). The faster the feedback loop, the quicker we learn.

- Honor and embrace diversity, both cultural diversity and diversity of thought. Learn from everyone and every place.

RESPONSE STRATEGY 10

Identify Sharks, Carps, and Dolphins

Understanding how members of the team operate allows a leader to help them perform better and respond to resistance according to who is involved. The "strategy of the dolphin" developed by authors Dudley Lynch and Paul Kordis (1988) can be a useful tool when thinking about people you work with. This strategy identifies people in conflict as having the characteristics of sharks, carps, or dolphins.

Sharks move straight forward trying to assert their beliefs and opinions on everyone else. They tend to be fixated on their way or the highway. When confronted, they tend to attack, create chaos, or divert attention. They are vulnerable because they tend to be inflexible in their thinking.

Carps, on the other hand, tend to be victims. They tend to run away from any conflict and prefer to get out or give in. They will play nice but usually do not follow through and would rather keep others from winning so they do not look bad. Carps believe in scarcity and believe they will never get their share of resources. They are vulnerable because they refuse to participate and may cause others to quit in frustration.

Dolphins keep their eye on the goal, seek win-win solutions, and are the most flexible thinkers. When something is not working, they will collaborate to create something positive: "You know dolphins are near if you are making progress when it long since should have ceased" (Lynch & Kordis, 1988, p. 20). In other words, if you look at a school or department and see many problems, yet the school is still somehow succeeding, dolphins are likely present. The next step is to find out who the dolphins are, support them, and invite others to join in. Dolphins make the best leaders, no matter what level in the organization they work at, and they can rally commitment from others. Dolphins are your best learners, and developing dolphins will give your organization a tremendous advantage in an uncertain world.

In conflict situations, the sharks eat up the carps. When they have eaten all the carps, sharks start fighting among themselves. Dolphins, by their collaborative nature, stay out of unproductive conflicts. With their flexible thinking, they can dodge around and overcome the straightforward, rigid attacks of sharks.

Here are eight mindsets from *Strategy of the Dolphin* (Lynch & Kordis, 1988) that help determine if team members are sharks or carps.

1. **There is only one way to play the game:** Sharks and carps both believe this. They know their roles and do not believe they have the power to change those roles.

2. **Only certain players can participate:** Carps feel like they don't belong and won't stand up for themselves.

3. **There must be winners and losers:** Sharks take this competitive mindset and try to stay on the winning side at the expense of others.

4. **Time is running out:** Carps often have the perspective that there's no use trying because the team won't be able to reach the goal in time.

5. **Rules are rules and cannot be changed:** Sharks are rigid thinkers and like to control the system; this is a strong indicator.

6. **Things are getting too serious:** Carps put on a façade, but do not really believe they can contribute. They are scared of negative responses, so they say what they think will satisfy others.

7. **People are playing to eat up time on the game clock, rather than to generate options:** This strategy of attrition is indicative of sharks, who take a survival-of-the-fittest approach.

8. **People are hiding future moves to keep others unprepared:** Carps doubt their own abilities and take this mindset to avoid showing weakness and being caught off guard themselves.

These questions can help determine what role a person might play when conflict arises in a work group. If you know the roles present in the group, you can proactively set norms that will create a safe environment and allow all team members to express their best thinking.

Differentiate Cognitive and Affective Conflicts

Some teams produce consistently better results while others become dysfunctional. This difference is often attributable to whether the team engages in cognitive conflict or affective conflict (Amason, Thompson, Hochwarter, & Harrison, 1995; Garmston & Wellman, 2016). *Cognitive conflict* refers to discussion and debate around differences of philosophy, research-based programs, and personal preferences. There might be disagreement, but it is civil and revolves around ideas, not the people themselves. Examples of cognitive conflicts might include the following.

- One elementary teacher prefers a phonics approach to reading because it is a parts-to-whole process while another has read that the whole-language approach yields better results.

- One middle school mathematics teacher wants to devote more time to fluency with computational skills, but other team members want to ensure students can solve real-world problems with mathematics.

- One member of a high school history team is concerned about a reduced emphasis on recalling the details of historical events; another teacher argues, "I want students to leave our school with a feeling of social responsibility, not just facts."

Cognitive conflict can increase trust, commitment, and respect for differences, leading to a better understanding of professionals' points of view.

Affective conflict, on the other hand, is personal and emotional. On teams that engage in affective conflict, members attack people rather than ideas. Someone might say, "you are just being stubborn" or "you're always so negative about everything." Affective conflict within teams can destroy relational trust, restrict honest discussion, and prevent progress, leading to less sharing of ideas. Table 2.2 compares the effects of cognitive and affective conflict on teams.

Table 2.2: Effects of Cognitive and Affective Conflict

COGNITIVE CONFLICT	AFFECTIVE CONFLICT
Better decisions	Power decisions
Higher commitment	Less commitment
More cohesiveness	Less cohesiveness
Increased empathy	Decreased empathy
More understanding	Destructive conflict

Source: Amason et al., 1995.

One way to guide teams away from affective conflict and toward cognitive conflict is to establish norms in initial meetings to agree on how everyone will work together. Expectations that collaborators honor each other's points of view and avoid personal attacks will help members participate more and express their educational beliefs. One set of norms I have used in most cases is from the work of Robert Garmston and Bruce Wellman (2016). Their seven norms of collaboration are as follows.

1. **Pausing:** Take a breath before responding to make sure you heard what was said.

2. **Paraphrasing:** Respond with what you think are the most important points (see Response Strategy 2, page 25).

3. **Putting inquiry at the center:** Ask questions rather than making judgments.

4. **Probing for specificity:** Ask about any fuzzy nouns, vague verbs, and universal quantifiers that you don't understand (see Response Strategy 1, page 17).

5. **Placing ideas on the table:** Make sure everyone has a chance to speak and feels safe sharing their opinion.

6. **Paying attention to self and others**: Notice your own reaction to the issues and observe others to see if they are reacting nonverbally.

7. **Presuming positive intentions:** Assume everyone has the best outcome in mind.

I often add an eighth norm, provide data, which was originally developed by Bill Baker and Stan Shalit (1991) as part of their "Eight Norms of Collaboration." Leaders can discuss cognitive and affective conflict and norms with teams in response to conflict, but they can also raise these topics proactively to prevent unproductive and harmful conflicts from arising in the first place.

RESPONSE STRATEGY 12

Name the Elephants in the Room

People in conflict often talk around issues instead of discussing the real problem. Teams and organizations pay a price for such passivity—time drains away and relationship quality deteriorates when people let things fester rather than addressing them directly. In education particularly, time and relationships are two of the most valuable non-renewable resources. A simple way to get to the point is to name the elephant in the room—to state the underlying problem, even if it is uncomfortable. As Sue Hammond and Andrea Mayfield (2004) point out in their book on naming elephants, "The real challenge is to decide which is more destructive: acknowledging the elephant to deal with it or ignoring it at your organization's peril" (p. 3).

To begin this conversation, ask, "What are the undiscussables in our organization?" Undiscussables make it impossible to talk about new trends or formulate creative ideas to address those trends. Team members perceive that silence on these issues will maintain calm and protect their status within the organization. Unfortunately, these are short-term benefits with massive long-term consequences. As an example, think of the Space Shuttle Challenger disaster, which killed seven astronauts. It is well documented that individuals knew of the engineering flaws in the O-rings and risks of launching in colder weather but failed to address the problems in favor of protecting themselves and the organizational image (Howell, 2019; Rogers Commission, 1986). There are times when the pressure to conform while in a group is very high. Without the trust to have authentic conversations, individuals generally will conform.

Different people within an organization may have different points of view on the elephants in the room, so it is important to discuss them as a group. Here are some questions to use to create conversation in your work group (Hammond & Mayfield, 2004).

- What are our undiscussables?
- What is it we did not talk about today that we should have?
- What information do we have that contradicts our current beliefs?
- How many people spoke up to present information that challenged the status quo at our last meeting?

These questions provide team members with opportunities to name elephants and bring up topics that they might usually feel pressure to keep quiet about. Note that this is only the beginning of the conversation; continue the dialogue with people from all levels of the organization in order to surface underlying assumptions about the elephants (Hammond & Mayfield, 2004). Based on this exchange of information, the team can generate possible reactions and solutions.

Consider the phrase "no news is good news." In reality, it may be more accurate to say, "no news is bad news." If you are not receiving any news, it may be because people may not feel safe to bring concerns to their leaders. This is why organizations end up with surprises instead of preparing for a new future when the environment changes—employees were too scared to name the elephants. Developing a culture of psychological safety, where people feel secure sharing information, concerns, and solutions, is an ongoing process. That norm has to be honored and reinforced or people will fall back into "go along to get along" mode. Hosting a conversation where you explicitly ask your team to discuss the undiscussables is an excellent start, but works best early to set the tone and norms of our meetings to enhance a collaborative culture. As mentioned in chapter 1 (page 18), if you can't find out what the real problem is, you can't solve it. Worse, you solve the wrong problem, and the true issue never goes away. Name the elephants, get the problem right, and save time and energy for yourself and the organization.

Summary

This chapter presented several methods for responding to conflict within teams. When people work closely together on a regular basis, they need ongoing strategies to develop collaboration and cohesion. Leaders can use this chapter when conflicts occur or as a preventative measure. Leaders can help set the vision of a group, define outcomes, and help the small group determine metrics for assessing progress. Depending upon the make-up of the small group, the leader can use the concepts from this chapter to assess individual roles, how the individuals relate to other group members, and how the members function as a team. Are they teaming, or are they a group of individuals?

Many of these small-group strategies are adaptable also to individuals and larger groups. The next chapter addresses strategies most applicable to individuals. After all, small and large groups consist of individuals. Leaders will often need to respond to individual actions and their potential influence on groups.

CHAPTER 3

Strategies for Working With Individuals

Basic human needs are . . . at the
heart of every conflict. . . . We all want to be
appreciated, respected, acknowledged.

—The Tao of Negotiation

While schools are typically organized around teams, there are plenty of instances of individual interaction and conflict. Individual conversations with staff and students can be difficult ones— performance evaluations and behavioral infractions, for example. If a parent comes to see a school leader, it is usually because he or she is upset about something. Because such interactions can become heated, responding to conflict with an individual relies on managing emotions and maintaining respect and esteem between parties. This chapter focuses on the following strategies for working with individuals.

Response Strategy 13: Counter Emotional Blackmail

Response Strategy 14: Discern Individual Priorities

Response Strategy 15: Make Others Feel Heard

Response Strategy 16: Utilize the Three Fs

Response Strategy 17: Defend Yourself Strategically

Response Strategy 18: Manage Up

Response Strategy 19: Standardize Difficult Conversations
With the FRISK Model

RESPONSE STRATEGY 13

Counter Emotional Blackmail

A parent calls the administrator to request a schedule change for her daughter. She does not specify a reason, and the administrator knows from experience that the issue, most of the time, is that the student's friend is in another class or has a different lunchtime. The administrator has balanced classes the best he could with the constraints of the schedule and accommodations of student preferences, and so declines to change the schedule. He explains to the parent that, during the first week of the term, teachers are trying to establish norms and create class unity, and changing this student's schedule would disrupt that process. He also mentions that one change usually means at least two changes because switching one class causes a ripple effect.

The parent continues to demand the change, simply trying to get what her daughter has asked for. The administrator declines again, explaining that making an exception for her daughter will start the telephone ringing as other parents request changes for their children, creating more unsettled classes. The parent pressures the administrator further. The administrator declines a third time. The parent now threatens to go to the superintendent or school board.

At this point, the administrator has two options:

1. Give in—Comply with the parent's demand and change the student's schedule

2. Dig in—Hold his ground and refuse the change

If the administrator gives in and complies with the request, chances are there will be a lot of similar requests, making it harder and harder to say no. Class sizes will likely get out of balance. More students in a class means less time from the teacher for each student.

If the administrator digs in, chances are the parent will go over his head to a higher authority. Depending on the support from those above him, the administrator has to weigh the risk. If his supervisors have supported him in the past, it is easier to dig in, knowing that the higher-ups will also refuse the request. If, however, the cultural norm is to give parents everything they want, the superintendent or board will probably overrule the administrator. Sometimes the administrator has to decide where to take a stand.

· · · · · ·

Emotional blackmail, as the term itself suggests, is a situation in which a person threatens to make things more difficult for you if you do not give in to his or her request. It quickly becomes a downward spiral (Forward, 2019). Figure 3.1 displays a visual depiction of this process.

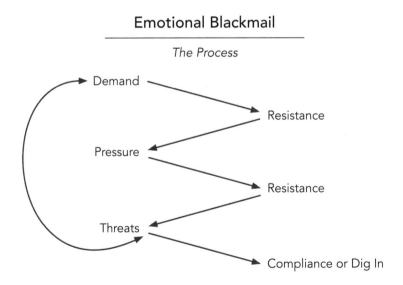

Source: *Adapted from Forward, 2019. Image © 2020 by aha! Process, Inc. Used with permission.*

Figure 3.1: Emotional blackmail.

To avoid this downward spiral, Susan Forward (2019) recommends clarifying the demand that the other person is making in the first encounter. Recall the first foundational skill, use specific language (page 17). In the vignette at the beginning of this section (page 58), the administrator should find out the reason that the parent is demanding her daughter's schedule be changed, making sure it is not just because of a friend or a lunchtime. Getting the reason out in the open will make it much harder for the parent to bully the school leader into a decision. If the other person gives a reason that seems vague or suspect, do not be afraid to push back. For example, a parent might reference incompatible learning styles as a reason to move a student to a different class. Ask questions about the student's learning style and the teacher's instructional style. It will become clear very quickly whether or not this is a valid reason.

Clarifying the demand up front may save you time and emotional energy. Otherwise, you may be faced with the choice of give in or dig in. Neither choice is much fun. Sometimes it is best to give in and make an exception; other times it is best to stand firm. The following scenarios exemplify both options.

- A parent is asking for a schedule change for his or her child; the student was in this teacher's class last year, and it did not go well. It is probably best for the student and the teacher to try something different in this case.

- A teacher resists implementing a new curriculum for his subject area. When discussing this with the administrator, he indicates he has always taught his own way, posits that it is the students who changed, and questions who made the decision to change the curriculum. When the leader calmly counters these points, the teacher implies he will activate his colleagues to resist the change as well. The leader must then decide whether to give in and make an exception for this teacher or stand firm and potentially face a larger backlash.

- A student who was the lead in the school musical intentionally uses a curse word over the PA system while reading an announcement about the show. The assistant principal suspends him for the day—which happens to be opening night of the musical. The musical director asks the principal to override the assistant's decision, threatening to go to the parents and site council if the student is not allowed to perform. The principal has to decide to back the assistant principal's decision or acquiesce. In this case, the understudy performed opening night.

In some cases, the leader should dig in and stand his or her ground. In my own experience, I once opted to dig in and refuse to change a student's schedule when a parent called me to ask. This parent happened to be the spouse of a school board member, as well as a nice person whom I knew not to be confrontational or hostile. I declined to change the schedule. However, a short while later, I got a call from the superintendent asking if I could make the class change for that student—the parent had gone over my head. I responded, "How many other requests for class changes do you want?" He said that the parent had promised not to tell anyone else about the change. "Regardless," I countered, "there will be thirty students from the class the student comes out of and thirty from the class the student goes into that will know. It will take about forty-two seconds for the word of the change to get around the school." I continued that I could not overload another teacher and that there would be more requests, all of which I would deny since we were already a week into the term. The superintendent said, "Don't make the change. I'll handle the parent."

RESPONSE STRATEGY 14

Discern Individual Priorities

One staff member felt her colleagues undervalued her. She was very talented, built great relationships with students, and had high levels of support with parents. She was very good at collecting and using data to improve her teaching. She was excellent at helping kids learn scientific concepts. Yet, when it came to serving on committees, taking leadership roles, and contributing to school improvement plans, she opted out of most things. I was curious about why a very effective teacher tended to be so isolated and prone to withholding her leadership potential.

As I thought about the situation, it occurred to me that perhaps this teacher did not feel that her status as an effective, experienced teacher was being recognized by her colleagues. This is an example of status being part of her identity. She did not feel like she could make decisions or contribute beyond her own classroom because she had not been at the school very long. As I started to stop by her classroom more, talk to her about education, and ask what she was working on to teach kids better, she started feeling noticed. Eventually, I invited her to be on the leadership team and the site improvement team. We were able to leverage her expertise, she felt engaged, and the school benefited.

· · · · · ·

When managing individual staff members, especially in conflict situations, leaders must consider the person's own priorities and values. Identifying what is important to a person and what motivates him or her helps assess the best point of intervention. One model of individual priorities is *SCARF*, an acronym devised by David Rock (2010).

- **Status:** Concerns about one's importance relative to others
- **Certainty:** Concerns about predicting the future

- **Autonomy:** Sense of control over events
- **Relatedness:** Sense of safety with others
- **Fairness:** Perception of an equal exchange between people

Once you know which of the five values a person identifies with most closely, that information provides a way to reduce conflict with others and can be used for team building. The following sections provide guidelines for working with individuals who prioritize each element of the SCARF model.

Status

Those who prioritize status value feeling important relative to others. They want recognition from their colleagues and to be acknowledged for their service, knowledge, or expertise. Where deserved, increasing leadership repertoire or identifying professional goals will motivate these staff members to perform. In the vignette at the beginning of this section, focusing on status moved the relationship in a positive direction, and the school benefited from the teacher's expertise.

Certainty

Many educators are looking for certainty in these times of constant change. When certainty is the issue, leaders can ask, "What hasn't changed since you started teaching?" or "What hasn't changed in the school or community?" Being able to identify the constants, as well as how they have adapted to changes and continued to succeed, staff members gain a positive perspective. Teachers are continually and automatically adapting to changing standards, demographics, and needs of business. Leaders occasionally have to make these small adjustments and successes visible to them. In addition, look for ways to support their need for some constant guideposts—their values, their beliefs about students, and continuity of the curriculum.

Autonomy

Highly efficacious, talented staff usually want some autonomy. Often, they are very experienced and used to depending on their own skills. Micromanaging these professionals is not helpful. Paying attention to them is helpful. Ask questions, visit their classroom, and give them as much autonomy as you can. These people are prime for mentoring for newer staff, becoming informal leaders in the school, and driving initiatives they feel are important. However, their sense of personal efficacy can cause challenges when they have to collaborate on teaching and share materials and strategies. You might hear, "I'm better off with *my* kids in *my* classroom. I don't want to spend the time with others." That is a strong signal that you'll need to support the individual in contributing to a team.

Relatedness

In most schools, there is a high number of staff members who value relatedness. They are social architects—this is what makes them good with students, relationship building, and school culture. When a staff member values relatedness, the social collaboration is primary. These staff tend to be the ones who join social committees, lead sunshine clubs, and otherwise work to make the school feel friendly and familial. They will contribute to the well-being of the school for both students and staff. If relatedness is their number one priority, make sure you keep providing connections for them with each other and leaders. Honoring their participation and commitment to the community of learners is important, and it builds the trust necessary to help them expand their instructional prowess as well.

Fairness

Staff who are motivated by fairness are always looking to the leaders and the system to make sure they feel treated equally. Each teacher may have a different way to assess fairness, and the only way to find that out is to talk to the person. Fairness can mean how the individual is treated compared to the rest of the staff, how the leaders treat him or her, or what the district contract provides for staff. There are times when people want everyone to be treated exactly the same, and there are times when individuals want to be treated differently because of special circumstances. Again, if fairness is the top of the list, it is important to have a conversation about what is fair in that individual's mind. Leaders need to set boundaries and they have to know when to deviate. Leaders consider extenuating circumstances at times when necessary.

Using the SCARF model and identifying a colleague's priority can make a big difference in how you approach conflict with the person, conflict between colleagues, and groups within the school. Departments and grade levels also have collective identities. Apply this strategy and see if it can help move effective programs forward.

RESPONSE STRATEGY 15
Make Others Feel Heard

Marshall Rosenberg (2003), author and founder of the Center for Nonviolent Communication, explains that in the fast-paced, uncertain world, people make judgments. Often, they make these judgments quickly, without all of the necessary or relevant information. In disagreements or conflict situations, emotions can blur the lines between making judgments about ideas and making judgments about people. Unless dealt with constructively, the issue of *what* becomes the issue of *who*, and people may end up focusing their frustration on the person instead of the issue at hand. Figure 3.2 (page 66) shows the negative loop teams can get caught in.

In these automatic response loops, one person makes assumptions and judgments about what the other person is saying, thinking, or

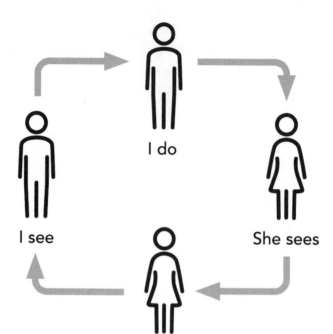

Figure 3.2: Automatic response loop.

doing instead of actually listening to him or her. She then responds to her own assumptions, making it clear that she has not heard the other person. The other person reacts in kind, and the cycle continues. The following list presents some typical behaviors and responses that can contribute to a feeling of not being heard.

- **Advising:** "I think you should . . ."
- **One-Upping:** "That's nothing; wait until you hear what happened to me."
- **Educating:** "This could turn into a very positive experience for you if you . . ."
- **Consoling:** "It wasn't your fault; you did the best you could."
- **Storytelling:** "That reminds me of the time . . ."
- **Shutting down:** "Cheer up. Don't feel so bad."

- **Sympathizing:** "Oh, you poor thing . . ."
- **Interrogating:** "When did this begin?"
- **Explaining:** "I would have called but . . ."
- **Correcting:** "That is not how it happened."

When people in conflict respond in this manner, they miss the emotional cues that drive much of the conflict in organizations. They keep going through the same issues over and over with no resolution. Tempers rise, emotions take over, people make hurtful statements, and the relationship deteriorates.

To make others feel heard, frame the conversation around two questions.

1. What is it that each of you need?
2. What would you like to request of the other in relation to these needs?

Notice the first question focuses on what you each need. The second question allows each party to state what they are requesting of the other person. This helps clarify what deficiency is causing the conflict and gives insights into each other's thoughts and feelings. These questions are effective if you are facilitating a conversation or if you are party to it.

I have found these two questions important as I join a team or work with an existing staff. These questions can be used with teachers, assistant principals, and so on, but let me give you an example involving another critical person—the principal's administrative assistant. When I come into a new situation, within a day or two, I set up a meeting with my administrative assistant. We get to know each other personally and discuss how we will work together. I ask, "What do you need from me to be successful?" and then say what I need from the assistant. Then, we talk about specific ways I can support my administrative assistant and vice versa. Keep in mind this is an ongoing conversation, perhaps once a week for the first month and then monthly for the first year. It is a time to show each other we are listening, try our best to make the other person successful, and make midcourse corrections if something is not working as well as we would like.

Listening to people is critical for solving differences. Once you listen, you are able to paraphrase (see chapter 1, page 25). Once the messages are clear, you can begin to find ways both sides might get some of their wants, or at least some small, quick wins. Knowing what each other wants, the conversation can shift to developing a pathway to get results.

(**16**)

RESPONSE STRATEGY 16

Utilize the Three Fs

A general education teacher comes to see the principal. He says he is upset about the new policy that students with special needs will be assigned to general education classrooms, including his. He is afraid he will end up spending most of his time with the special needs students and less time on other students. He requests having the special needs students removed from his class and put in a class by themselves.

The principal responds, "I felt that way at one time—that all special needs students should be in their own classroom. Now I feel they should be in mainstreamed as much as possible because I found out special needs students show more academic growth when they are in mainstream classes than when they are separated out."

• • • • • •

Leaders often need to respond to negative statements, impossible suggestions, and ideas that are just flat-out wrong. In these situations, you need to stop the negative and turn the conversation in a positive direction. Telling the other person he is wrong or bluntly denying a request does not solve the conflict. First, let the person vent and tell you his or her concerns before responding. If you skip this step, the other person may feel ignored or put down. Then, respond using this three-part approach.

1. Honor the other person's point of view.
2. Promote a new thought or plan.
3. Provide new information that reframes the issue.

An easy way to remember these three parts and present them in a discussion is the three Fs: I **felt** that way [restate the other person's perspective], but now I **feel** [state your way of thinking] because I **found** out [provide new information]. As long as you include all three elements, the order in which you state them is not particularly important. For example, you might present your reframing information before stating your new thought or plan. The following examples demonstrate this strategy.

- A group of parents wants extracurricular athletics and marching band to count toward the school's physical education credit requirements. They want to make room in their children's schedules for academic electives by removing their need to take the required physical education and health class. The six-period day makes it difficult to fit all the courses parents want for their kids.

  Response: At one time, I felt physical education and health were not as important for kids. Now I feel the required class is an absolute necessity because I found out that physical health increases mental health, and a universal physical education class teaches cooperation with all types of people. I also learned that direct instruction on health topics such as alcohol, drugs, depression, and so on is critical for keeping students healthy and teaching them to make good decisions.

- At a meeting of the school's administrators, a group of staff members comments that parents are the biggest problem for school leaders and staff.

Response: I felt that way at one time because I thought since I had the license to teach, it is my class or my school, and I will make the rules. Now I feel that parents are partners in learning. The closer the connection between parents and school, the better for the students. I found out that the more the school listens to parents, takes their concerns seriously, educates parents through back-to-school nights and newsletters, and brings parents into the leadership process, the more support we receive from parents. We are the professionals, but it is important to hear their point of view.

The power of this strategy is that it offers a new belief based on new information. It helps the complainant understand why the leader may be denying a request or choosing a different option. Not every conflict can end in agreement, but at least it can end amicably.

RESPONSE STRATEGY 17

Defend Yourself Strategically

In a middle school grade-level team made up of five individuals, each teacher fit a different role. One person never wanted any conflict and would do anything to smooth over any difference of opinion—she was a placater. A second person, a typical blamer, took the view that there was no problem that wasn't someone else's fault—it was the kids, the families they come from, the lack of funding, and the list goes on. A third person on this team was a nonemotional computer. He only looked at data and was almost devoid of the social-emotional connections that are an important part of learning. Fourth, a distracter. Any time the team needed to discuss hard issues he would use humor or diversion. Finally, a leveler—in response to any issue that threatened her, she would lash out and play the victim.

This team needed a lot of help working together due to their individual behavior patterns. The principal would have to help each individual modify his or her role to contribute to actively working together.

- For the placater, the leader had to make sure she was able to talk in team meetings, put her ideas on the table, and not take responsibility for everyone else's feelings.

- For the blamer, the leader had to monitor his language and his nonverbal communications. The leader would ask someone else in the group to synthesize what the blamer was saying. The summaries helped remove emotion and retain any valid and appropriate thoughts.

- For the computer, the leader honored the use of data to monitor students. The leader worked with him to bring more social-emotional learning into the advisory program for middle school students.

- For the distracter, the leader would meet with him prior to the meetings to go over the agenda. The leader gave him the responsibility of keeping the team on topic during meetings. That kept him and the team generally on task.

- For the leveler, the leader gave her a journal. Her challenge was to write down the response she wanted to make first. That gave some time between internal reaction and verbal response.

· · · · · ·

When conflict arises, you must recognize what kind of attack you are facing in order to formulate your defense accordingly

(Evans, 1996). I recommend Virginia Satir's (1972) five behavior patterns as an effective framework for this process (see also Sommers & Zimmerman, 2018).

- **The placater:** This person will do anything to resolve conflict, even acquiesce.
- **The blamer:** This person wants to find fault and someone to blame.
- **The computer:** This person approaches conflict with facts and data, not emotions.
- **The distracter:** This person will raise multiple issues to divert focus from the main conflict.
- **The leveler:** This person feels there is a one-up and one-down power dynamic, and his or her goal is to bring you down.

Do not respond in the same pattern that is coming toward you. Adopting the other person's pattern keeps him or her locked in the same role instead of creating a new pathway out of the dysfunction. Once you identify the role, or take your best guess, you can help by asking questions and creating action plans. The following list provides some suggestions for how to respond to each of these behavior patterns.

- The placater
  - Make sure that suggestions will work over the long term. Placaters may present short-term solutions to resolve immediate conflict more quickly.
  - Help identify the values involved. A placater might abandon his or her ethics just to end the problem.
- The blamer
  - Identify all parties involved (including the blamer) and have them accept responsibility for their contributions to the conflict.

- Focus on actions that you and the blamer can each take moving forward. Assigning tasks in advance can help prevent blamers from inducing guilt and coming back to you later with other issues.
- The computer
  - Insist on objective data. Computers may be adept at manipulating data to suit their arguments. Research a topic rather than making a quick decision.
  - Aim for the heart. I was working with a teacher who was extremely content knowledgeable. The students believed he did not care about them, only their answers on tests. Since computers tend not to be emotional, in tough cases you can counter them with phrases such as, "If this student was your child, how would you like the teacher to respond?" He got tears in his eyes, and it changed his demeanor. He was not perfect but tried harder to show empathy.
- The distracter
  - Pick one or two of the problems the distracter mentioned and get some momentum. Try asking, "Out of all the issues you have talked about, which one or two are the most important to deal with?" You cannot solve everything at once.
  - Do not try to solve issues that are beyond your control. Some professional conflicts are made more complicated by problems in the distracter's personal life. Focus on what can be resolved in the school setting.
- The leveler
  - Try to elevate the leveler's point of view toward gaining consensus and common goals, rather than winning.

- Help the leveler use language that mediates conflict, rather than black-and-white statements. For example, "Here is how my point of view can add to the decision to make it better."

The following are categories of questions that can help you craft a solution to the different patterns (Costa & Garmston, 2002).

- **Efficacy:** What do you think you can do to get a different response? What have you done in the past that has helped you work out difficult issues?

- **Flexibility:** How might you do something different or respond differently to get a different response?

- **Consciousness:** What behaviors are the most troubling? Which one would you like to try to resolve or manage first?

- **Interdependence:** Who else could you ask for an idea on how to manage this issue?

(**18**)

RESPONSE STRATEGY 18

Manage Up

Leaders are constantly managing people: those who report to them, those to whom they report, and those who are their peers. In addition, leaders also have to manage themselves. Dee Hock, the founder of Visa, said in a 1996 interview in *Fast Company* magazine (Waldrop, 1996) that leaders should spend 30 percent of their time managing those who report to them, 15 percent managing peers, 15 percent managing up to those to whom they report, and 40 percent managing themselves (see also Raffoni, 2008). Unfortunately, many leaders put most of their thought and effort into oversight, neglecting their relationships with the people above them.

It is essential to be aware of one's direct supervisors. In one district where I was a building principal, the superintendent loved athletics, specifically football. When I would come into the office and say, "I have some research I would like to share with you," the superintendent would roll his eyes and look for a distraction. I learned to keep his attention by speaking his language: "Think of yourself as the quarterback, and the principals are your linemen." This is an extreme example, but it illustrates how you must consider the personality and management style of your supervisors to best work with them.

Later in my career, I worked for another superintendent who was more of a micromanager. Micromanagement can be disheartening and make you feel like your knowledge, skills, and talents are not being valued. Compliance-based systems can be difficult to work in for long periods of time, especially for very experienced and talented leaders. I found a strategy from Michael Dobson and Deborah Singer Dobson's (2000) book *Managing Up* called the five-fifteen report. It is a review of the past week and upcoming events or concerns written for one's supervisor. It should take fifteen minutes to write and five minutes for the supervisor to read. My five-fifteen reports were simple bulleted lists and contained major events of the past week, upcoming concerns with my recommendations, and future events in the weeks ahead. When I made a habit of submitting these weekly reports, I received fewer questions from my superintendent on a daily basis. He felt informed and in the loop despite the fast pace of the school.

Collaboration is a balance of communication and trust. If your supervisor leaves you alone, that might be nice in the short term. However, in the long term, having no feedback or communication can make you vulnerable to making the wrong decisions. At the same time, being micromanaged can cause resentment and feelings of inadequacy or lack of trust in your judgment. As Peter Drucker, leadership expert, said, "You don't have to like or admire your boss, nor do you have to hate him. You do have to manage him, however, so that he becomes your resource for achievement, accomplishment, and personal success" (as cited in Dobson & Dobson, 2000, p. xix).

To summarize, the following guidelines will help you manage up.

- Speak your manager's language. Communicate the way he or she prefers to communicate.
- Offer information regularly. Keep your manager in the loop to prevent tendencies toward micromanagement. If you provide updates proactively, your manager will not have to pester you.
- Build trust through communication. Even if your manager is not your favorite person, communicating with him or her builds trust and will make your job much more pleasant. Over time, he or she will trust you to do your job well with less oversight.

RESPONSE STRATEGY 19

Standardize Difficult Conversations With the FRISK Model

After receiving several complaints about negative comments made by a teacher in department meetings, the chairperson met with the individual. After two more meetings and feedback from the chair, the issue moved to the administrative level. The main issue was that the negative comments were affecting the department morale such that nobody wanted to meet or contribute ideas because of negative rumors that would arise about the person raising the issue.

The administrator in charge of the department met informally with the individual a couple of times, but the negative behavior persisted. Finally, the administrator decided to elevate the conversation to ensure the teacher understood the facts, rules, and impacts of the situation, as well as to make suggestions for changing behavior and share knowledge about options going forward. It is always important to create a plan of correction before further administrative decisions are made. The administrator outlined the issues and put a plan in writing. The teacher in this case did make the necessary changes to make team meetings more hospitable.

$$\cdots\cdots$$

Occasionally, as a leader you will have to have a hard conversation with someone when his or her performance is not meeting expectations. Try starting with informal chats, but if those do not lead to improvement, it is time for a more standardized conversation. One structure I recommend is FRISK, which stands for facts, rules, impact, suggestions, and knowledge. I learned this strategy from Diane Zimmerman, former superintendent in Petaluma, California. We included this in our book *Nine Professional Conversations to Change Our Schools* (Sommers & Zimmerman, 2018).

- **Facts:** Provide evidence of the conduct. What have team members said, and what are they feeling about working together with this individual? Remember, feelings are facts, and emotions can increase or decrease collaboration.

- **Rules:** Explain the rules that govern the situation. What are the norms in the school and department for working positively together? What is the current state of affairs and working conditions, and what are the expectations for professionals?

- **Impact:** Describe the impact of the individual's behavior on the work environment. State the effects on the team, the individual, and the school culture. You might also state what might result if the behavior continues.

- **Suggestions:** Make suggestions for how the individual can improve his or her behavior and clearly state future expectations. Leaders will always have the responsibility for suggesting a plan of correction. Left alone or unchecked, the administrator can be held accountable for not clearly stating expectations for positive behavior. This can derail further disciplinary processes if needed in the future.

- **Knowledge:** Share knowledge about the employee's rights in disciplinary situations. Always include what options the individual has. Where applicable, the leader must be open to union or association representation. The process has to be fair, or you may forfeit further action if required.

The FRISK process is not in place of disciplinary procedures. FRISK is designed to get a change in behavior prior to formal disciplinary action. You may never have to use this process, but it is still important to have it in your repertoire in case less intensive interventions are not working.

Summary

The strategies presented in this chapter can help reduce resistance and manage conflict with individuals. Whether the conflict is between you and a stakeholder, two members of your staff, or another pair of individuals, these strategies will help you respond appropriately to move forward when a conflict stops progress. A leader does have a responsibility to facilitate understanding, maintain relationships, and move sticky situations toward a workable environment. Understanding the person, the problem, and effective communication tactics is essential. In a human-centered field like education, individual conflicts can erupt at any time. How you respond to resistance will be a model for the organization and have a great impact on the emotional health of the school culture. The next chapter will turn to ways to manage larger groups where the number of people requires fitting communication and negotiation techniques.

CHAPTER 4

Strategies for Working With Large Groups

Between what I think, what I want to say, what I believe I'm saying, what I say, what you want to hear, what you hear, what you believe you understand, what you want to understand, and what you understood, there are at least nine possibilities for misunderstanding.

—François Garagnon

As important as managing resistance and conflict with individuals and small groups is, there are times leaders have to address difficult issues in large groups. The larger the group, the more chances for misinterpretation, disagreement, and conflict. While you can also modify the strategies from previous chapters, the following strategies are more conducive to larger groups.

Response Strategy 20: Deliver Bad News Productively

Response Strategy 21: Negotiate on Principles

Response Strategy 22: Overcome the Knowing-Doing Gap

Response Strategy 23: Prevent Mobbing

Response Strategy 24: Investigate Positive Deviance

Response Strategy 25: Facilitate Controversy

Response Strategy 26: Recognize the Value of Opponents

RESPONSE STRATEGY 20

Deliver Bad News Productively

I came out of retirement to fill in for the principal of a middle school who had quit in the middle of the fall semester. The superintendent told me the district was in good financial shape with no funding issues, but by spring, budget cuts were imminent. The responsibilities of the principal include leading the process to cut budgets with the staff while maintaining positive relationships. Fortunately, I had built relationships with most of the staff during the six months before cutting the budget.

I received the budget cuts in the morning, and the same day I called a staff meeting after school. I did not want the information flowing from the central office to the staff. Timeliness and honesty are extremely important in maintaining trust. I did my best to give the bad news in a calming, forthright manner, communicate that I was on the teachers' side, and reduce the uncertainty in the school. At the end of the presentation, I asked if there were any questions. The only comment I got was, "Thank you for giving us straight information quickly so rumors did not divert us."

Then the team leaders and the administrative staff worked on the best ways to reduce the budget and staffing. We kept the whole school informed after each budget meeting—rumors waste emotional energy. In the spring of my second year, I was doing the same thing because of more budget cuts. When the teachers arrived, they knew exactly what was going to happen. It was a difficult time, but we remained united as a staff.

· · · · · ·

All leaders will have to deliver bad news on occasion. Sometimes the bad news is a problem or error of your own making. In these cases, revisit Response Strategy 3: Accept Responsibility (page 26). In other cases, you are only the messenger—you did not create the bad news, but it is your responsibility to deliver it. Perhaps the most common example of this in schools is when a principal must announce state or district budget cuts to his or her staff. Of course, you do not want the bad news to ruin your relationships with the people receiving it. The key to delivering bad news without creating animosity is using verbal and nonverbal communication to depersonalize the information and distance yourself from it. This helps maintain a positive tone in your interactions with the recipients, allowing you to address the bad news as a team. Michael Grinder (1997) wrote about this process in his manual *The Science of Non Verbal Communication*. The process is valuable for presentations to staff, conferences with parents, and meetings with other administrators.

- **Provide visuals:** Make sure the news or information and any associated data are on a white board, chart paper, projector screen, or other visualization where people can see it.

- **Stand off to the side:** Stand off to the side of the visualization so you are not in the direct line of fire with the bad information. Stand at a ninety-degree angle to the information offered—standing with your back to the audience does not work and fully facing the audience conveys vulnerability.

- **Direct attention with your eyes:** While talking about the process or the solution, look at the audience to keep the focus on the positive relationship. When talking about the bad news itself, focus your eyes on the information (that is, your visual display) to direct the group's eyes there as well. Do not look at the group. If you look at the group, they will look at you while you are telling them what they do not want to hear and they may unconsciously connect you with their negative feelings.

- **Speak in the third person:** Say "the data" or "the information" or "the report." Do not say "my budget," "my staffing," or "my data." When you personalize it, you become connected to it.

- **Separate the problem from the solution:** As soon as you are done giving the bad news, while keeping your eyes focused on it, take two or three steps to one side and then look at the audience. You have now separated yourself from the information. When you are a few steps away, say, "We [gesture to them and to yourself] are going to figure out how to deal with this [point to the data] together."

- **Use credible and approachable tones of voice:** When speaking about the data or report, use a credible tone of voice. Keep your voice in a lower, more monotone range, and pitch your voice down at the end of each sentence to communicate in definitive statements. When you move away from the data, start speaking in an approachable voice, modulating pitch and tone up and down more to convey friendliness. Use a more open stance and hand gestures.

- **Be specific:** State the exact amount of budget cuts or precisely how often a student has been sent to the office and why. Do not use vague phrasing like, "We are going to have some budget cuts and reduce some staff." Uncertainty leads to rumors and panic. Say, "We are cutting $34,725.83." Say, "We are cutting 3.6 full-time equivalents."

By putting space between you and the bad news, you can direct the group's attention back to the information. You, then, are part of the group (rather than the enemy) wanting to figure out what to do about the bad news.

The vignette at the beginning of this section illustrates how this strategy might look in a staff meeting. This strategy is also particularly useful in parent conferences, where there might be bad news about grades or behavior. The same elements are important. Display grades or discipline referrals on a sheet of paper (rather than keeping it in a gradebook or private memo) so the parents can see it. Place the paper off to the side, closer to the parent, and keep your eyes focused on the report so the parent looks at the report. Speak in specific terms about the issue and how the student can improve in class or in the school—it is the behavior or the grades that are bad news, not the student. Use a credible voice while providing the difficult information. When finished, lean back or shift your body to separate yourself from the report and use an approachable voice, saying "How can we work together to help John do better?"

RESPONSE STRATEGY 21
Negotiate on Principles

Negotiation refers to discussion between two parties seeking to reach some form of compromise. In schools, leaders may need to facilitate negotiations between groups of staff members who have differing ideas about practices to implement. However, this strategy is also particularly adaptable for use with teams and individuals. It includes any difference of opinion from two people disagreeing to formal contract negotiations. There are mainly three types of negotiations.

1. **Hard:** Take a tough position and don't budge.
2. **Soft:** Prioritize the relationship and avoid conflict, even if you have to give in.
3. **Principled:** Be hard on issues, soft on people.

In principled negotiation, the parties can focus on goals and results rather than who is good and who is bad. This is a five-step process that is popular in business settings but applicable in education and beyond (Fisher & Ury, 2011).

Step 1—Separate the People From the Problem

Both parties in a negotiation have to respect each other, but if they focus on people, chances are the emotions will drive negotiations. I have seen more agreements break down because of emotion than on the merits. A process called *structured controversy* can be used to separate the people from the problem. In structured controversy, each person takes the other's side for a time. Taking the other side can give a perspective not normally visible when you think only from your point of view. By depersonalizing the different positions and separating the people from the problem, both sides can look at solving the problem rather than taking it personally and getting emotional. This approach works well with staff and even students.

Step 2—Focus on Interests, Not Positions

There is a story about two sisters who argued over an orange. They finally decided to cut the orange in half. One sister ate only the fruit inside her half. The other sister used only the rind from her half for a cake she was making. If they had both initially expressed what they wanted the orange for—in other words, focused on their interests rather than their positions—they both would have gotten more of what they wanted (Olsen & Sommers, 2003).

If both sides talk about their reasons, purposes, and desired outcomes, they can start seeing overlap. Identifying where each side agrees or where interests are mutually compatible can be a source of progress even if both sides have been stuck. Starting to work collaboratively on what both sides want can build cooperation and trust.

Step 3—Invent Options So Both Get Something Positive

In a fixed-pie or zero-sum negotiation, there is a winner and a loser. Every benefit to one party is a detriment to the other party. When this happens, the issue might be solved, but the relationship can suffer. Therefore, beware of ending the negotiation prematurely without exploring as many options as possible. For example, when trying to secure funding for an initiative, the school budget is likely a fixed pie—any program that receives funding takes that money away from other initiatives. Rather than rejecting a new initiative or defunding an existing one to support it, a leader might look to grants from outside organizations, fundraisers, alumni gifts, and so on. Perhaps there is a little-known additional funding source from the state. Be creative and leave no stone unturned.

Step 4—Use Objective Criteria

Looking at a negotiation from only your point of view tends to be biased. We all look at things through our own lens, often making assumptions about one way to do something. Teaching is no different. The college you attended, the professors you learned from, the professional development activities you've attended, and the school and district administrators you've worked with probably influence your beliefs. Finding an objective standard is helpful in that both sides can agree that an outside party might have a better, more objective view.

For example, perhaps a group of educators is reviewing new research-based instructional strategies and debating which ones to implement in the school. Two factions have formed, each with its preferred option, and they are having trouble making a final decision. One option for finding an objective criterion would be to look closely at the design of each study if one of the strategies has a stronger backing for its results. Perhaps the teachers discover that one of the studies had a small sample size and the experiment only lasted an hour. This weak research design provides an objective standard.

Step 5—Find the Best Alternative to a Negotiated Agreement

This step presumes the first four have not worked and the possibility of no deal is on the horizon. Each party must have a minimum result that they can accept. In your negotiations, it is best to decide what your bottom line is before the negotiation, in case discussions reach this point. In the most extreme cases, this might mean answering the question, What are you willing to get fired for? Or, What are your non-negotiables that would make you resign? These are not easy questions to answer, but it is better to think about the answer before you are in a crisis or in a hard negotiation. If you cannot solve the negotiation, what are you willing to live with? This is sometimes referred to as *BATNA*: best alternative to a negotiated agreement (Fisher & Ury, 2011).

In most negotiations, each side has their non-negotiables and a list of things they are willing to give up. You know when you have reached the bottom line. Sides dig in. If there is no agreement, then walking away may be the best alternative to a negotiated agreement. Sometimes the values underlying a negotiation are so important that a group will not give them away. If you are willing to walk away from a bad agreement, the other side sometimes will come around. Of course, this is not a sure thing. Only walk away if no deal is better, from your perspective, than a bad deal and your side is willing to take the consequences.

When no deal is an option, you have more power in the process. Of course, most negotiations do have to reach some kind of resolution. Different negotiations have different amounts of flexibility. Obviously, for infractions around weapons, drugs, and violence, there is no room for negotiation. However, in rule infractions for minor student behaviors, teacher evaluations, and board policies there is likely some room for adjustments. When there is a negotiation over budgets, staffing, or internal or external conflict, decide on your BATNA and see if the four preceding steps can help manage or resolve the differences.

RESPONSE STRATEGY 22

Overcome the Knowing-Doing Gap

One of the most discouraging feelings in schools is that of constant talk without action. Education as a field is constantly progressing.

Clientele, neighborhoods, technology, and other factors are always changing. The latest research recommendations call for teachers to update their practices. When a new principal, superintendent, or other leader comes into the system, he or she brings new ideas, new consultants, and new materials. The constant change is difficult to keep up with, so it is not uncommon for educators to be aware of new thinking but fail to act on it, especially in systems with high leadership turnover. If new administrators come in every two or three years, staff may begin to suffer from *repetitive change syndrome* (Abrahamson, 2004)—they go into their rooms, work with students, and ignore new initiatives. They know things will change again soon and their efforts will not be recognized or sustained.

All this uncertainty contributes to the knowing-doing gap. The following five elements describe specific reasons that gaps arise in organizations between what people know and what they do (Pfeffer & Sutton, 2000).

1. **When talk substitutes for action:** When groups talk about change but take no action to implement the ideas, energy is depleted. Without follow-through, staff learn to believe no substantive change will happen, trust goes down, and people will wait the change out. It is better not to present a new initiative if there won't be follow-through to implement it.

2. **When memory is a substitute for thinking:** Times change, staff change, and demographics change, constantly creating a new environment. When a leader presents a new idea, they might get a response like "We tried that five years ago." Adverse memories can set teachers against new thinking, even if there is strong evidence it could work in the current system. Another way memory can substitute for thinking is when leaders forget to continually build support for key initiatives. A principal once brought

me in as a consultant. Her concern was that people were questioning the school's focus, which was Spanish immersion. I asked, "When did you become a Spanish immersion school?" The principal's response was, "Eight years ago." My second question was, "How many new staff have joined the school in the past eight years?" Her head went down as she said over half the staff had changed. She had the memories of the consensus- and culture-building activities, but the new staff did not.

3. **When fear prevents action:** Change is risky. Staff must feel safe to implement new ideas and possibly fail at first. I worked in a district where the superintendent said at the opening principal meeting, "If you can't raise test scores, find another job." This established a culture of fear in which principals were too worried about keeping their jobs to try anything that might actually improve test scores. The human resources director was heard saying, "You can't fire your way to excellence," and left the next year. In eight years under this superintendent, over 80 percent of the principals in the district left or retired. Test scores did not improve; the only result was huge cultural upheaval for the schools.

4. **When measurement obstructs good judgment:** In 1995, David Berliner and Bruce Biddle wrote *The Manufactured Crisis*, which describes how education in the United States has over-prioritized test scores. Tests were never designed to rate students, teachers, or schools. In many systems, the focus on testing and measurement obscures good thinking about what is best for students. There is little time left for formative assessment, responsive instruction, critical thinking, social-emotional learning, and inclusive teaching when high-stakes exam scores are the priority. Schools purport that they want to prepare students for life and the workforce, but the best companies want creativity,

innovation, grit, collaboration, trust, and so on, which most schools do not measure. For more on this topic, I highly recommend *50 Myths and Lies that Threaten America's Public Schools* (Berliner & Glass, 2014).

5. **When internal competition turns friends into enemies:** While tying compensation to productivity may work in manufacturing contexts, Daniel Pink (2009), Daniel Goleman (1998), and Edward Deci (1995) all present research indicating that external rewards do not motivate knowledge workers. Factors like achievement, recognition, and growth generate the best work leading to innovative practices. There have been several school districts that started paying teachers for higher test scores or growth rates, only to find out that the competition destroyed collaboration and created divisions among the staff (for example, RAND Corporation, 2007).

It is one thing to identify the knowing-doing gap. It is quite another to find ways to overcome this difficulty. The following list provides some possibilities to help close the gap.

- **Share why before how:** Make sure the staff know and understand the purpose behind any program or initiative. Without the why, people tend to be reluctant to invest time and energy.

- **Emphasize action over plans:** Try something, even if it doesn't work out. Experiment and then report your findings and lessons to others. Share what works and what doesn't work given the context you are working in.

- **Make mistakes:** Make mistakes and allow others to do the same. Celebrate those mistakes because they mean people are trying. Mistakes happen as people try different ways to improve. As mentioned previously, fear of making mistakes increases the knowing-doing gap; psychological safety is key.

- **Beware of false analogies:** Rarely are two situations the same. We still can learn from what others do and provide additional options. For example, if you learn a strategy from a colleague at another school, acknowledge that its application will not work the exact same way at your school, but do not let that stop you from taking action.

- **Measure what matters:** Make sure your school or district is measuring the right things. What you measure will become your priority. Content acquisition is easier to measure via testing than attitude, creativity, and motivation, but easier does not mean better. If you want creative, self-assured students who work well with others, think in terms of possibilities, and are willing to share their ideas, how will you measure that?

- **Send a message with your actions:** What do leaders do? How do they spend their time? Leaders signal what is important. If the principal stays in the office doing budgets, scheduling, and staffing, students and staff will not know who this person is. When relationships are so important, where does the leader spend his or her time? That sends a clear message. People watch everything!

- **Cultivate trust and collaboration:** Team members who contribute to each other's learning, add suggestions for improvement, and trust each other are more able to collaborate to overcome the knowing-doing gap. One way to cultivate this is through a regular meeting in which everyone shares current tasks and challenges (Sheridan, 2018). All staff gather in a circle, and each person or small group reports three things: (1) what they are working on, (2) what they are learning, and (3) where they might need help. As soon as the circle is completed, people connect with each other to share knowledge and solutions to challenges that were mentioned. The whole process takes about fifteen to twenty minutes.

Too many conversations about what the problem might be and how to solve it result in little or no action. Leaders, assess the knowing-doing gap. Ask questions to find out—if we know what to do, why aren't we doing it?

RESPONSE STRATEGY 23

Prevent Mobbing

Most educators can identify the bullying that goes on between students. Bullying is destructive to students, reducing the emotional safety in schools. Being a bystander contributes to bullying and further isolates the bullied student. The Violence Prevention Initiative (2010) finds 21–49 percent of youth report being bullied in a given year. Over 70 percent of youth have been bystanders to bullying. Ninety percent of students in grades 3–5 have felt sorry for students who are bullied. However, when students demonstrate bravery and stand up for the bullied student, the bullying often stops.

Like students, staff members can experience a type of bullying that is sometimes called *mobbing*. Mobbing occurs when several staff members do not like a certain person for some reason, and they enlist others to tolerate or participate in ganging up on that person by ignoring him or her and intentionally misinterpreting his or her intentions. The constant negative treatment wears down the victim, causing him or her to doubt his or her own competence and ability to perform the job. The way bullies treat the victim, and the victim's own self-doubt, often lead others to assume the isolation is a result of a defect in the victim's character. Research by Heinz Leymann (1990) found that the work culture creates circumstances that label victims as difficult to work with. In the age of technology, bullying and mobbing have become even more commonplace because a person can promote a negative attitude toward another professional without publicly saying anything. Using technology as a shield has, unfortunately, made mobbing easier.

There are five phases in the mobbing process (Leymann, 1990; Leymann.se, n.d.), which progress toward expelling a person from an organization.

1. **Conflict:** Some critical events of contention, committed directly or indirectly in subtle or obvious ways
2. **Aggressive acts:** Emotional and psychological assaults on the dignity, integrity, credibility, and professional competence of employees
3. **Management involvement:** The problem is misinterpreted, ignored, tolerated, encouraged, or even instigated by the management of the organization; by not taking action, management colludes with the attacks.
4. **Branding as difficult or mentally ill:** Identifying and naming the victim as the problem; portraying the victimized person as being at fault
5. **Expulsion:** The victim is isolated.

Mobbing can only occur if management condones it. The leader or administrator is responsible for actively making the work environment a safe place. The following are ways to address this in a school.

1. Establish a vision statement with positive values that the school wants to encourage.
2. Establish procedures for reporting and confronting bullying behavior for the organization.
3. Define professional responsibility to the psychologically safe environment that supports and enhances learning for staff and students.

4. Clearly define the process that will be used when an event is reported, including investigation and consequences (involve human resources in setting this process). Commit to addressing conflicts honestly and thoroughly.

5. Communicate the school's values in an ongoing basis to signal clarity and commitment.

If bullying or mobbing is happening, leaders must take action. My colleague Diane Zimmerman, retired superintendent and former human resources director, told me that the main antagonist must be confronted (personal communication, July 2017). The leader must ensure that one bad apple (or even a few) does not spoil the barrel.

RESPONSE STRATEGY 24

Investigate Positive Deviance

Jerry Sternin, developer of positive deviance as an approach to social change, went to Vietnam in the 1990s to try to help starving children (Dorsey, 2000). When he arrived, the officials who greeted him said, "You have one month to make progress, or we will send you back." Jerry decided that he should only ask questions, not make statements or judgments. The following conversation ensued.

Jerry: Are there any healthy children living in these villages?

Officials: Yes, but we don't care about them.

Jerry: Why are there healthy kids living in the same conditions as the malnourished children?

Officials: We don't know.

Jerry: Can we find out by asking the parents what they are doing differently?

That started the positive deviance model. There were positive examples—someone doing something successful—and they were deviant—different from the norm. This is an example of an asset-based rather than deficit-based approach.

Once Jerry and his team determined the successful strategies that parents of healthy children were using, they did not write a report of the results and pass them out to all the parents. They did not post the strategies on the sides of tents and telephone poles. Instead, they convened a conversation between the parents of the healthy children and the parents of the malnourished children and let them transfer the information. Jerry knew that the parents would listen to people from their community rather than people from outside it. Despite his record of success with similar issues, he did not have credibility with that community. As he said to me later, "Do you think [they] would listen to two white people who just got off the plane?" Point taken (personal communication, July 2005).

. . . . . .

In every school, there are staff members who are getting positive results with the same students about whom other teachers say, "Nothing works with these kids." Using the positive deviance approach, leaders can focus on which behaviors are getting good results and how that happens. The process is as follows. Notice it is about asking questions, not giving advice or research.

1. **Define:** What are the problems, solutions, and desired outcomes?

2. **Determine:** Where can we find examples of desired outcomes?

3. **Discover:** What are the unique practices of those who are successful?

4. **Design:** How can we design and implement an intervention?

5. **Discern:** How will we know if it is effective?

6. **Disseminate:** How can we make this knowledge or practice accessible and scale up?

This is a collaborative approach to solving problems and conflicts that honors the knowledge and experience of staff and stakeholders. As another example, a central office administrator was assigned to help student achievement in an underresourced urban district. The school system had very low scores compared to state averages. On visiting schools, the administrator discovered there were teachers in the most challenged schools who were being successful. She held meetings to find out what those teachers were doing differently to get better results. Those schools and staff became sites to visit for others in the district. The administrator leveraged those teachers to share strategies with their colleagues and lead summer professional development sessions.

Figure 4.1 displays a list of questions that leaders can use to learn from positive deviants in their schools and districts.

- Who are the positive deviants in our school? Which teachers are making greater progress with the students who struggle in other classes?
- What are these teachers doing differently? Which unique practices do they identify as critical to their success?
- What are the students doing differently in these classrooms?
- What can I do to amplify and accelerate these positive deviations? How can I spread this information that might help others in the school?
- Which teachers might benefit from spending time with colleagues who display positive deviance? Who is willing to learn new ways or expand their repertoire?
- How can I support positive deviants in continuing to experiment and try new ideas? What do these teachers say they need from their leaders?

Figure 4.1: Learning from positive deviants.

*Visit **go.SolutionTree.com/leadership** for a free reproducible version of this figure.*

Facilitate Controversy

A new high school principal arrived on the job in the middle of a conflict: some of the staff wanted to move to a four-period block schedule, and an equal number of staff wanted to stay with the six-period day. The majority of parents were against a change. The district office said it was a site-based decision, so it was up to the new principal to facilitate the decision process (and take the heat for the choice).

In the fall, the principal assembled interested staff on both sides of the issue, along with some of the parents, to work as a committee on a recommendation. The two groups of staff were each formidable, with good teachers on both sides, and the parents had a history of being involved in school decisions. The principal knew that a respectful process in which all opinions were heard was of the utmost importance. The school would implement whatever decision the committee came to. Though not everyone would get their way, the process had to maintain collegiality and avoid creating a schism in the staff or community.

The principal facilitated the decision with input from all sides. Staff groups, which included people on both sides of the issue, would visit the two other high schools in the district that had already shifted to a four-period schedule. These subgroups would issue a report written together with the pros and cons of changing. After gathering and sharing all the relevant information with the entire school community, there would be a faculty vote. The principal established a threshold of 70 percent. If the vote for the change did not reach that margin, the school would remain on the six-period day. The principal knew that such a consequential decision should not be made by a simple majority—a 51–49 result would create a schism.

The principal informed the parent committee members that parents would not be included in the vote. The parents were understandably upset, but the principal calmly explained that the staff were the ones affected by and responsible for implementing the decision. While parents, of course, have a vested interest in what goes on in the school, teachers are the experts and will have to live with the change for longer. Another complication arose when the principal learned that several faculty members were retiring at the end of the year. The principal put the question to the committee, which decided that only those staff members who were committed to staying at the school would vote.

Sixty-four percent of the staff voted for a four-period schedule. Though a majority, this did not meet the established threshold of 70 percent, so the school stayed with the six-period schedule. Not everyone celebrated, but it was a decision all could live with.

· · · · · ·

It is not uncommon for school and district leaders to encounter situations in which they must mediate a conflict between two factions within their staff. Disagreements are tolerable, but you must facilitate skillfully to avoid creating enemies. If staff members do not like or trust each other, it will be difficult for them to work together in the future. There are essentially four options when facilitating a disagreement: (1) collaborating, (2) forcing, (3) adapting, and (4) exiting (Kahane, 2017).

If appropriate, you can guide the two sides to collaborate and make a decision (as illustrated in the vignette). Consider the following guidelines.

- Listen to all stakeholders. People need to be heard, or they may immediately sabotage the decision.
- Be transparent about the process and how the decision will be made, otherwise people may feel manipulated.
- Start the investigation of the issue. Find examples of where a solution exists and what the obstacles are.

- Present discoveries to all stakeholders.
- Make a decision based on the pre-established process.
- Make the decision public and state the reasons behind it.

If necessary and you have power of position or the political capital, you can impose a decision by force. However, rest assured there will be backlash. Sometimes you galvanize the resistance, which may not be the best way for the good of the organization. Be sure you can live with the consequences of forcing a decision before you make a unilateral choice.

If you cannot live with forcing a decision and the resulting behavior, consider adapting the options and coming to a compromise both sides can live with. This path is not available if the two options or opinions are incompatible or mutually exclusive. The final option is to consider exiting the issue. This is not always possible—sometimes a decision is required, but sometimes no deal is the best deal. Here are the tenets of this strategy.

1. **Embrace conflict and connection:** When smart people do not agree, connect them and see what happens. Sometimes the process of working through an issue collaboratively brings people together.

2. **Allow groups to gather and discuss their own information:** Research and investigation are important to collaborative decision making. Rather than providing groups with the information you think they need, let them discover it for themselves.

3. **Encourage perspective taking:** If each faction defends its own position, the process is likely to result in deeper divisions. Have each side present pros and cons of both positions. They will better understand each other and be more likely to support the eventual decision.

4. **Set ground rules:** Set ground rules at the beginning of the process. Clarifying the process at the beginning saves time and hard feelings at the end. If the process is not clear at the outset, you run the risk of accusations of bias, blaming, and finger pointing from the losing side. People are more accepting when they know the ground rules up front. They may not like the final outcome, but they know the rules.

5. **Experiment to find a way forward:** Try something—anything. Do not wait for the perfect way to do things. Bring people together and design a process.

6. **Face into the storm:** As the story of the buffalo (page xi) teaches, turn toward the problem and walk into it. Turning away might mean you never get past the thunderstorm.

Many issues can be difficult to navigate. The goal is to resolve or manage different beliefs or problems without long-term damage to the relationship. Sometimes this is not possible. Using these strategies will minimize relationship problems in times where a decision has to be made.

RESPONSE STRATEGY 26

Recognize the Value of Opponents

Whether you are a new leader or an experienced leader, you will have different relationships with different staff members. If you are new, it is important to find out as quickly as possible what type of working relationship you are likely to have with each staff member. If you are an experienced leader, staff have already decided how they view you. It takes consistent behavior change to alter that view—I am reminded of the saying that friends come and go but enemies accumulate.

Organizational consultant Peter Block (2016) wrote a book titled *The Empowered Manager* in which he presents a two-factor scale for categorizing relationships with staff members (see figure 4.2). The axes are agreement and trust. If a staff member has high trust and high agreement with you, they are probably your *ally* on most things. If another staff member does not trust you and does not agree with most things you do, they are probably your *adversary*. Staff members who do not trust you but are getting what they want (agreement) are your *bedfellows* on an issue. If they trust you but do not necessarily agree with you, they are *opponents*.

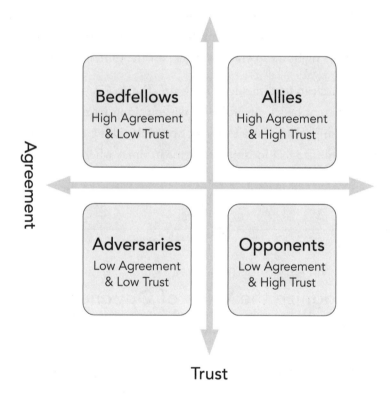

Source: Adapted from Block, 2016.

Figure 4.2: Agreement and trust.

Various leaders will have differing opinions on which quadrant is most important. Of course, your allies are important. Bedfellows will be with you or against you depending on whether or not it serves their interests. Adversaries take up a lot of time if you try to convert them, which may not work no matter what you do. I believe the most important group is your opponents. They are people who trust you but will tell you honestly if they think you are wrong. As a leader, you need these people around you. I identify these people as the ones I will check with before rolling out a new idea. They tell me the truth, whether or not I like it.

Table 4.1 describes practices that are helpful in collaborating with people in each quadrant.

Table 4.1: Best Practices for the Four Quadrants

QUADRANT	BEST PRACTICES
Allies	• Make sure they are with you on projects or policies. • Maintain the relationship. Do not ignore them just because they trust and agree with you. • Ask for their feedback on planned ideas and find out what concerns they have.
Adversaries	• Find out whether or not they really are adversaries. • Paraphrase their position as you understand it. Give them a chance to restate their position. • State the reasons for your decision even though they may not agree. • State your plan to move ahead with the best intentions for the greater good. • Don't ignore them but don't let them dominate your time.

continued ➤

Bedfellows	• Check with them to see if they agree with you on projects or policies. • Try to reach agreements on the planned implementation and your expectations. • Be aware they may be hard to manage because they may change their minds depending on others who may be trying to win them over.
Opponents	• Maintain the relationship. • Check their perception of projects or policies and their opinion. • Have them work with you in problem solving. • Don't mistake an opponent for an adversary.

Summary

The strategies in this chapter are focused primarily on the larger groups that a leader must address. When presenting or responding to large groups there is more of a chance that there will be a surprise. The more people, the more likely an unexpected issue will arise. Even though you cannot predict every possible exchange, the more prepared you are with response strategies, the more confident you will be. Moreover, as a result, the group will be more confident that you can manage an uncertain situation. Having a repertoire of conflict management skills will provide competence and confidence to respond to resistance. Although this chapter focuses on larger group issues, many can be adapted to small groups. Being able to deliver bad news to a large group, maintaining your values during difficult times, and facilitating collaboration on a large scale are part of a leader's responsibility. You will be tested. Be ready to negotiate and navigate through turbulent times.

At this point in the book, you may be wondering, What if none of these strategies are working? The next and final chapter will address some strategies of last resort.

CHAPTER 5

Strategies for When Nothing Seems to Work

> That's the hard thing about hard things—
> there is no formula for dealing with them.
> —*Ben Horowitz*

Some problems are unsolvable. Michael Pacanowsky (1995) calls these "wicked problems." While leaders can solve tame problems relatively quickly and equitably, they must constructively manage wicked problems, or face the resulting reduced collaboration and unproductive workplaces. These problems do not have clear ways to solve them and involve managing the issue. Two qualities will help you identify a wicked problem: (1) the two conflicting sides are interdependent, and both are needed for a good school; (2) the issue is ongoing and requires an ongoing solution. For example, consider a common conflict between two approaches to teaching reading: phonics versus whole language. Phonics proponents believe strongly that teaching the parts-to-whole method is best. There is research to support this. The whole-language teachers are convinced it leads to better results. There is research that supports this approach as well. This is a common argument in schools and districts, with each side committed to their approach. This conflict is a good example of a wicked problem—selecting one option is not feasible because both approaches have their strengths and greatly benefit students.

The following strategies are helpful when nothing you have tried seems to work.

Response Strategy 27: Balance Polarities

Response Strategy 28: Approach Terminations Realistically

Response Strategy 29: Recognize and Respond to Verbal Abuse

Response Strategy 30: MOVE Underperforming Employees

RESPONSE STRATEGY 27

Balance Polarities

A new principal came to a school where the staff consisted of about 65 percent experienced teachers and 35 percent who were relatively new to the school or the profession. The experienced teachers perceived the newer teachers as naïve and overly optimistic, saying they needed to stick to tried-and-true methods. The less experienced teachers argued, "If these more experienced teachers would try something new, maybe we could do better for students." The divide intensified, and issues became polarized. Neither side wanted to negotiate. The experienced teachers took the position that the younger, less experienced teachers just didn't know how to teach yet. The less experienced teachers took the stance that the more experienced teachers wouldn't try new things and were stuck in the past. The principal needed to find a way to balance both groups' strengths.

· · · · · ·

Breathing is a good metaphor for understanding polarities and why choosing one is impossible. If a person was somehow excellent at inhaling and very bad at exhaling, on average she would be a decent breather, but in reality, she would die. Resolving the polarity of inhalation and exhalation by choosing one or the other does not work; each side has both limits and essential benefits. It is a process, an ongoing flow of shifting emphasis from one to the other and back again. Managing this polarity requires choosing both inhaling and exhaling.

As a more practical example, consider the school in the preceding vignette. Imagine a school that had only experienced teachers or only inexperienced teachers, and it quickly becomes clear why a school needs both sides of this polarity. There are some good things that come from experience, such as instructional prowess, political savvy, formal and informal leadership, and connections to the community. However, flexibility and willingness to try new teaching strategies often fade later in a teacher's career. Inexperience has some negative connotations, but newer teachers also tend to have lots of energy, new ideas, and willingness to take on extra assignments. The point is that there are plusses and minuses to both sides, and schools and districts need both to be successful. This polarity also requires ongoing management as staff members retire, leave for other jobs, or join the team.

Figure 5.1 (page 106) is a tool that leaders can use when balancing a polarity. The leader fills in the benefits and disadvantages of each pole with input from stakeholders on both sides. Once filled out, it should be posted in department offices, the teachers' lounge, or wherever is most visible to the relevant parties.

This serves as a visual reminder of the goal to spend as much time as possible in the upper quadrants to get the best of both sides. The ideal is to stay within the positive loop represented by the figure eight in the graphic. Any time the team drops into the lower quadrants, reassemble the team and figure out how to get above the midpoint. When a team sees behaviors based on each side's fears, the positive attributes from the other sections of the map can lead

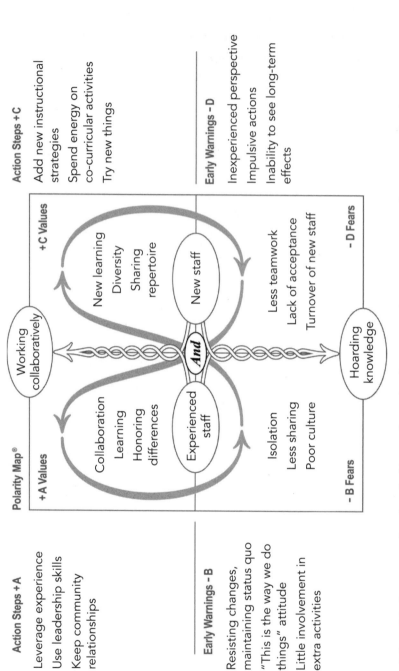

Action Steps +A

Leverage experience
Use leadership skills
Keep community
relationships

Early Warnings - B

Resisting changes,
maintaining status quo
"This is the way we do
things" attitude
Little involvement in
extra activities

Action Steps +C

Add new instructional
strategies
Spend energy on
co-curricular activities
Try new things

Early Warnings - D

Inexperienced perspective
Impulsive actions
Inability to see long-term
effects

Polarity Map®

+A Values

Collaboration
Learning
Honoring
differences

Experienced
staff

Working
collaboratively

And

+C Values

New learning
Diversity
Sharing
repertoire

New staff

- B Fears

Isolation
Less sharing
Poor culture

- D Fears

Less teamwork
Lack of acceptance
Turnover of new staff

Hoarding
knowledge

Source: Polarity Map® is a registered trademark of Barry Johnson & Polarity Partnerships, LLC. Commercial use encouraged with permission. Complete sourcing and attribution guidelines are available at https://www.polaritypartnerships.com/certification-licensing-1#licensing-and-sourcing

A public library of editable and downloadable Polarity Maps® are available at www.polarityresources.com.

Figure 5.1: Polarity management.

to better results. When dropping to the lower left quadrant, the answer is usually to counteract it with elements from the upper right quadrant. Dropping to the lower right, look for answers in the upper left. For example, if there are problems associated with having less experienced staff, leaders should look to engage their more experienced staff or hire staff members who bring a wealth of experience to the team.

Some of the common polarities in schools include the following.

- **Content versus process:** Is it more important for teachers to be content experts or instructional experts?
- **Working independently versus working as a team:** Do students learn better individually or in groups?
- **Whole language versus phonics:** Should students learn the meanings of whole words through stories or learn letter-sound correspondences and sound out words?
- **Computational skills versus everyday mathematics problems:** Should students learn algorithms and practice equations or focus on word problems and mathematical thinking?
- **Top-down leadership versus shared leadership:** Should principals manage by edict or form leadership teams and make all decisions collectively?

RESPONSE STRATEGY 28
Approach Terminations Realistically

Removing unsuccessful staff members is one of the most difficult parts of leadership, but it is essential to the well-being and efficacy of the rest of the team. Will Felps, Terence Mitchell, and Eliza

Byington (2006) published research on the organizational effects of "bad apples." When one person demonstrates negative behaviors or does not contribute, the rest of the team is likely to exhibit anger, mood changes, and reduced trust within the group. Felps and colleagues "found that productivity is reduced by thirty to forty percent by having one 'bad apple' on the team" (as cited in Sutton, 2017, p. 145). As Robert Sutton and Huggy Rao (2014) say in their work, "bad is stronger than good" (p. 217). Bad behavior has higher consequences than what those being good can do to counteract it.

Resolving these issues is not easy, and it is important for the organization. What makes working with bad apples even harder is there is no recipe or sure way to solve this. Ben Horowitz (2014) says that successful executives and managers "make the best move when there are no good moves" (p. 59). The only certainty is that turning away or procrastinating usually makes the issue worse. In other words, if you have decided that a person is destructive to the organization, address it immediately. Of course, you try improvement goals first. Once it is clear that person is not going to change, they must leave the group. As a leader, occasionally you encounter a person who either cannot or will not change. Once you have tried multiple interventions to encourage behavior that is better for colleagues, students, and community, you may have to decide to make a change in assignment or, in tough cases, help them leave the organization. Tackle the issue head on, and do not delay. You owe it to your team to protect them from continued damage.

Also, remember not to take this personally. If you have given time to change, been honest about the negative behavior, and offered clear corrective steps that go unmet, it may be time to pull the plug. Early in my career, I thought I could change other people's behavior through my caring and skill by coaching for excellence. I now know that was uninformed optimism. After I gained more experience, I moved to informed pessimism. Finally, with even more experience,

I am now at pragmatic realism—dealing with situations as they are and making the necessary decisions that help the mission of the school or district work. If you are unsure of your judgment on these matters, consult your critical friends and people you trust around you. Without people who will tell you the truth, you can fall victim to seeing everything through rose-colored glasses.

Here are some points from Horowitz's (2014) book, *The Hard Thing About Hard Things*, to consider when terminating an employee.

1. Be resolute—know what the final outcome is going to be. Once you make the decision to move a person out (probably in concert with a superintendent or human resources director), keep the end goal in mind.

2. Don't delay—if you have made the decision, do it. The longer you wait, the more the situation deteriorates, and the harder it is to make the call.

3. Be clear about the reasons, the corrective plan, and the result. I advise writing down these elements. First, it helps you prepare. Second, a meeting is emotional. With the plan written out, you can refer to the list to make sure you cover everything.

4. Make sure this is about the group, teamwork, and the negative impact. Be careful not to degrade the individual as a person. Focus on the lack of fit with the school team, effects the person has on the community, and so on.

5. Give options for moving on. Be respectful and positive by giving some recommendations for the future.

Removing someone from the school or organization is neither easy nor fun. It is the price of leadership. Failing to act when action is necessary will have a negative impact on the rest of the team. Your colleagues will see your inaction and turn their energy to protecting themselves rather than take abuse. Quoted in *The Hard Thing About*

Hard Things is Jim Barksdale who said, "We take care of the people, the products, and the profits—in that order" (as cited in Horowitz, 2014, p. 98).

Recognize and Respond to Verbal Abuse

Despite the old adage, words can sometimes cut deeper than any physical attack. Negative comments stay with the victim longer because they attack one's intentions, values, and humanity—key elements of one's identity. As mentioned previously (page 36), a negative comment may have up to five times the impact of a positive one (Gottman, 2012).

Conflict and abuse are not the same thing. Verbal abuse is a violation of boundaries, beliefs, and humanity. Verbally abusive interactions consist of constantly invalidating the victim's reality. The comments send the message that the abuser has power over the victim, denying the victim's own personal power. The communication is about dominance—I am right, and you are wrong, and it is not going to change. Note that it does not have to be intentional to be abuse; many times the abusive person either does not know how he or she affects others or is not motivated to change. Regardless, everyone has the right to his or her personal power and to make the best decisions, contribute creativity, and exist in a positive culture. When there are disagreements between colleagues of equal status, a leader can act as a mediator with some of the strategies already mentioned in this book.

However, if there is a power differential (as explained in the introduction, page 7), disagreements can occasionally lead to abusive interactions. Common power differentials between staff include teacher and instructional aide, principal and teacher, or district administrator and principal. If the more powerful party uses that status for coercion, it will decrease trust, reduce creativity, and cause organizational trouble in working together. Table 5.1 displays some different kinds of abuse with examples and potential responses.

Table 5.1: Abusive Language and Responses

TYPE OF ABUSE	EXAMPLE	RESPONSE
Yelling or aggression	"If you don't change this grade for my child, I will go to the board of education! You'll be finished! You shouldn't have crossed me."	"I won't tolerate being snapped at or yelled at" (Evans, 1996).
Negative talk	"Do you know what she did the other night? She was drunk."	"There's no need to spread rumors or make character attacks—that's not relevant to what we're discussing."
Withholding	"I know some things about this situation, but I am not going to tell you."	"I am tired of this one-sided conversation. Tell me what you are thinking."
Countering	"I know that my way is better than yours."	"We have a difference of opinion. You have your reasons, and I have mine."
Discounting	"You don't know what you are talking about."	"Stop discounting my opinion." "Listen to my reasons and take my thoughts seriously."

continued ➤

Disguising abuse as a joke	"You take everything too personally. I was just messing with you."	"Is this a joke? I do not like to joke about serious matters. Let's talk when we can be direct and serious."
Blocking or diverting	"I am not going to listen to this. There are bigger problems to deal with."	"Give me the respect to look at me and listen to my suggestions."
Blaming or accusing	"It is your fault that we have terrible meetings and never get anything worthwhile done."	"Please stop accusing and blaming me. I don't like being talked to that way."

As a school or district leader, you must immediately address any instances of verbal abuse that you become aware of. Ignoring it or letting it go is tacit approval. Take a firm stand against inappropriate, unprofessional behavior of this nature. For example, one of my teachers directed profane language at one of her colleagues. I found out about the incident after school and called both teachers to my office the next morning. I also met with their department chair, who informed me there had been other such incidents between these two professionals and other colleagues. I brought in substitutes for every teacher in the department and had an extensive meeting with those teachers to confront how colleagues will treat each other. The message was loud and clear: we will treat each other as professionals. The department chair and the assistant principal in charge of that department were responsible for monitoring behavior. Our strong response in the face of unacceptable behavior also communicated to the rest of the staff that we would confront inappropriate and unprofessional behavior.

It is also important to note that you may experience verbal abuse directed at you as a principal. Perhaps you and your district administrator disagree on a particular decision, and he or she chooses to communicate in an aggressive, unprofessional manner. If the person you are talking to has positional authority, he or she has the right to make the final decision. You have the right to express your opinions, and you have a right to your own dignity. The responses in table 5.1 are appropriate, professional responses to someone who is belittling you in a workplace conversation. It is often appropriate to have a conversation with human resources or the abuser's manager. If you experience a pattern of abuse that your employers are unwilling to address, I suggest you consider looking for another position. Of course, nobody can tell you when you should take this kind of stand; it is your decision based on your circumstances.

RESPONSE STRATEGY 30
MOVE Underperforming Employees

A teacher with over thirty years of experience and nearing retirement was plagued by low enrollment in his classes. Given that the school had over eighteen hundred students, he should have been seeing numbers around one hundred and fifty, but he was only teaching about fifty students total. The complaints were that his class was boring—nice person, boring class. After working with this staff member for a year or two, it was apparent to the principal that not much was going to change.

With the approval of human resources and the superintendent, the principal added an in-school suspension supervisor position and assigned this teacher to this position. The teacher did not want to go; he had been teaching for thirty years, and finally said, "You can't make me." Right of assignment made it possible to involuntarily move the teacher to in-school suspension supervisory. He spent his last two years as an in-school suspension teacher. He then retired. The school hired a creative, energetic teacher in replacement and two years later had strong enrollment and high student achievement in the same classes.

. . . . . .

Sometimes a teacher or staff member is not bad—not doing anything immoral or against school rules, not causing problems within the staff—but also just isn't very effective in teaching students. When an employee is not performing, leaders can follow the MOVE acronym to consider alternative steps.

1. **Movement:** Give the person another assignment.
2. **Outplacement:** Consider other job options, including career counseling.
3. **Voluntary exit:** Help reduce logistical barriers for someone who wants to leave the profession.
4. **Evaluation and elimination:** Collect evidence to determine if dismissal is appropriate.

This is a progressive set of options; therefore, the first option to consider is movement to another assignment within the school.

Movement

Reassigning an underperforming teacher can give that person a new start. As demonstrated in the preceding vignette, a leader might take this step to reduce negative impact on students or simply to use staff more efficiently. The move might be to another assignment within the department, or another grade level, or another building. Before reassigning a teacher, check that he or she has the proper licensure for the new position. If the problem person is a school leader or administrator, he or she might be moved to a central office position, especially if the district is seeking to change the culture of the building. The hope is that the new role will be a better fit for the teacher or administrator where he or she will perform better and contribute more to the organization.

Outplacement

If movement to another assignment in the school or district is not an option or has failed, outplacement is another possibility. There are outplacement counselors that work with people to find another job or a better fit for their skills. When a staff member is not happy, and neither is the school, having the hard conversations with the person can open up other possibilities. I have used outplacement services to help a person transition from teaching to another job that might reignite the individual's passion. Outplacement counselors can also be extremely helpful when doing staff reductions due to budget constraints. Be sure to treat those leaving the school well and provide honorable closure if possible.

Voluntary Exit

Whether it be a lack of passion, feelings of inadequacy, or an objection to new directions, sometimes people voluntarily leave teaching. The desire to leave may become clear through diminished performance, and as a leader begins to discuss this with the teacher, the teacher might express that he or she would prefer to leave the profession altogether. When approaching this option, it is important to involve human resources. The leader must follow proper procedures and legal requirements. The teacher may want to quit but feel unable to because of losing health insurance or other logistical issues. Sometimes a buy-out or a severance package might be available; human resources can help you find possibilities that will be good for the individual and good for the district. Talk to people, find out what they want, and then see what is possible.

Evaluation and Elimination

When you have exhausted the other options, the only remaining step is to evaluate and eliminate an underperforming teacher. Evaluate comes first because, in most cases, a leader cannot fire a teacher without cause and evidence. You must evaluate the teacher, provide a plan of correction, and then hold the person accountable to it. Only after giving the teacher an opportunity to improve and collecting data that prove she has not done so do you have the right to eliminate her.

If you are in a union environment, evaluation is all the more important. During my first year of principalship in a new district, a union representative, Skip Olsen of the Minneapolis Federation of Teachers, gave me great advice: make the case, don't expect we will just sign off if you haven't followed the process (S. Olsen, personal communication, January 1996). The union exists to support and protect teachers; do not expect it to approve a dismissal if you do not provide clear evidence and make the case. It takes time, but it must be done.

So, after trying multiple ways to solve issues, MOVE might be where you end up. These are the last options. Leaders will always be held accountable for collecting information, having the hard conversations with staff, and making the appropriate recommendations.

Summary

This chapter highlights a key point from the introduction (page 15): nothing works every time. The strategies in the first four chapters represent a repertoire of responses that will help leaders manage most conflict, but there will always be some disagreement, conflict, or emotionally charged issue that will defy solution. The strategies of last resort in this final chapter provide options for when nothing else seems to be working. Moving a professional from a position is not easy. This takes time, respectfully conferencing with a plan of correction, written documentation, and courage. Even though moving or removing someone doesn't happen often, it is something leaders may have to do. Remember, "what you permit, you promote" (Kerfoot, 2009, p. 245). Some polarized conflicts cannot be resolved, only balanced and managed in an ongoing fashion. Some individual problems inevitably end in termination. Welcome to the world of leadership—it is essential to have as many of these tools in your toolbox as you can.

CONCLUSION

I believe that managing conflict is one of the most important responsibilities of a leader. Leaders must create safe environments so that teachers and students can do their best work. The strategies I've described in this book are the ones I use the most to accomplish this goal. Start by using the ones that feel right for you. The truth is that all of these will work, and none of these might work: "No single perspective holds all the answers. Any single idea taken too far can become destructive" (Joni & Beyer, 2010, p. xii). So, the larger your repertoire of response strategies, the more influence you will have to maintain physical, emotional, and social safety in the school or organization.

My final suggestion for you as you lead, learn, and lighten the load for yourself and others? Protect yourself. Stay FIT: *fight* the right fight, learn *improv* skills, and take *time* for yourself to renew your energy.

- **Fight the right fight:** Getting into unproductive conflicts wastes time, consumes energy, and causes more negative emotional focus in the school. So, before engaging, make sure the issue is the right conflict and worth fighting. Save time and energy by addressing problems as soon as they become apparent. If you can anticipate a problem and have some possible ways to solve it, you want to influence the issue at the earliest or lowest level. When conflict is necessary, set a positive example in how you engage (Joni & Beyer, 2010).

- Focus on creating the future. Right fights are not about the past.

- Pursue noble purpose. Go beyond self-interest.

- Fight fairly. Establish rules and do not alter them during the conflict.

- Turn pain into gain. Seek benefits for everyone, even those who oppose you.

- **Learn improv skills:** Your life as a leader is improvisation. You never know what lies ahead for the day. You can plan all you want—and planning is important—but something unexpected is always going to happen in the life of schools. As I watched the television show *Whose Line Is It Anyway?* I realized this represented my life as a principal. I started taking improv classes, and it was the scariest and best thing I ever did. Even though I was an experienced principal at the time, I learned a great deal about responding on the fly and making quick decisions when necessary. One of my best suggestions for leaders is to take improv classes.

- **Take time for yourself to renew your energy:** Spend time with family, significant others, or your group of friends— especially those who are not in the education business. Most professionals I know spend an inordinate amount of time at school and at school events. Yes, that is good for the school and community, but I encourage you to have a life outside your school or district office. As Suzanne Bailey once said, "You have to rest your tools" (S. Bailey, personal communication, December 1992). She meant that you have to step back, get some separation, and take a break from time to time. Even if you have to block it off in your schedule, make time to recoup your energy—"You can't give what you don't have" (Sala, 2016).

Remember the story of the buffalo (page xi) that opened this book. Walk toward the conflict, bring your skillset, and stay true to your values. You deserve a psychologically safe culture, the staff deserve it, and most of all, the students deserve it. Make learning happen.

REFERENCES AND RESOURCES

Abrahamson, E. (2004). *Change without pain: How managers can overcome initiative overload, organizational chaos, and employee burnout.* Boston: Harvard Business Review Press.

Abrams, J. (2019). *Swimming in the deep end: Four foundational skills for leading successful school initiatives.* Bloomington, IN: Solution Tree Press.

Amason, A. C., Thompson, K. R., Hochwarter, W. A., & Harrison, A. W. (1995). Conflict: An important dimension in successful management teams. *Organizational Dynamics, 24*(2), 20–35.

Anchor, S. (2010). *The happiness advantage: The seven principles of positive psychology that fuel success and performance at work.* New York: Crown Business.

Arbinger Institute. (2000). *Leadership and self-deception: Getting out of the box.* San Francisco: Berrett-Koehler.

Arrien, A. (1993). *The four-fold way: Walking paths of the warrior, teacher, healer, and visionary.* New York: HarperOne.

Autry, J. A. (1991). *Love and profit: The art of caring leadership.* New York: Avon Books.

Badaracco, J. (2016). *Managing in the gray: Five timeless questions for resolving your toughest problems at work.* Boston: Harvard Business Review Press.

Baker, W., & Shalit, S. (1991). *Eight norms of collaboration.* Presented at the Cognitive Coaching Leadership Training, South Lake Tahoe, Nevada.

Barrett, F. (2012). *Yes to the mess: Surprising leadership lessons from jazz.* Boston: Harvard Business Review Press.

Bates, M. (2015, April 30). *Bullying and the brain*. Accessed at www.brainfacts .org/thinking-sensing-and-behaving/childhood-and-adolescence/2015 /bullying-and-the-brain on May 19, 2020.

Bennis, W. (1997). *Managing people is like herding cats: Warren Bennis on leadership*. Provo, UT: Executive Excellence Publishing.

Berliner, D., & Biddle, B. (1995). *The manufactured crisis: Myths, fraud, and the attack on America's public schools*. Reading, MA: Addison-Wesley.

Berliner, D., & Glass, G. (2014). *50 myths & lies that threaten America's public schools*. New York: Teachers College Press.

Block, P. (2016). *The empowered manager: Positive political skills at work* (2nd ed.). San Francisco: Jossey-Bass.

Brinkman, R., & Kirschner, R. (2012). *Dealing with people you can't stand: How to bring out the best in people at their worst* (3rd ed.). New York: McGraw-Hill.

Brown, B. (2008). *I thought it was just me (but it isn't): Telling the truth about perfectionism, inadequacy, and power*. New York: Gotham Books.

Buckingham, M., & Coffman, C. (1999). *First, break all the rules: What the world's greatest managers do differently*. New York: Simon & Schuster.

Chadwick, R. J. (2013). *Finding new ground*. Terrebonne, OR: One Tree.

Clark, K. K. (1993). *Life is change, growth is optional*. Saint Paul, MN: Center for Executive Planning.

Cooper, R., & Sawaf, A. (1996). *Executive EQ: Emotional intelligence in leadership and organizations*. New York: Berkley Publishing Group.

Costa, A. L., & Garmston, R. J. (2002). *Cognitive coaching: A foundation for renaissance schools*. Norwood, MA: Christopher-Gordon.

Crum, T. (1987). *The magic of conflict: Turning a life of work into a work of art*. New York: Simon & Schuster.

Davenport, N., Schwartz, R., & Elliott, G. (1999). *Mobbing: Emotional abuse in the American workplace*. Ames, IA: Civil Society Publishing.

David, S. (2016). *Emotional agility: Get unstuck, embrace change and thrive in work and life*. New York: Avery.

Deci, E. L. (1995). *Why we do what we do: Understanding self-motivation*. New York: G. P. Putnam's Sons.

Dobson, M., & Dobson, D. S. (2000). *Managing up: 59 ways to build a career-advancing relationship with your boss*. New York: AMA Publications.

Dorsey, D. (2000). Positive deviant. *Fast Company*. Accessed at www.fastcompany .com/42075/positive-deviant on March 9, 2020.

Doyle, M., & Straus, D. (1976). *How to make meetings work*. New York: The Berkley Publishing Group.

Edmondson, A. (2012). *Teaming: How organizations learn, innovate, and compete in the knowledge economy*. San Francisco: Jossey-Bass.

Edmondson, A. (2019). *The fearless organization: Creating psychological safety in the workplace for learning, innovation, and growth*. Hoboken, NJ: Wiley.

Evans, P. (1996). *The verbally abusive relationship: How to recognize it and how to respond*. Holbrook, MA: Adams Media Corporation.

Felps, W., Mitchell, T., & Byington, E. (2006). How, when, and why bad apples spoil the barrel: Negative group members and dysfunctional groups. *Research in Organizational Behavior, 27*, 175–222.

Fisher, R., & Ury, W. (2011). *Getting to yes: Negotiating agreement without giving in* (Rev. ed.). New York: Penguin.

Forward, S. (2019). *Emotional blackmail: When the people in your life use fear, obligation, and guilt to manipulate you* (Reprint ed.). New York: Harper Paperbacks.

Fredrickson, B. (2009). *Positivity*. New York: Crown.

Friedman, E. (2007). *A failure of nerve: Leadership in the age of the quick fix*. New York: Seabury Books.

Friel, J., & Friel, L. (1999). *The 7 worst things (good) parents do*. Deerfield Beach, FL: Health Communications.

Garmston, R., & Wellman, B. (2016). *The adaptive school: A sourcebook for developing collaborative groups*. Lanham, MD: Christopher-Gordon.

Glaser, J. (2014). *Conversational intelligence*. Brookline, MA: Bibliomotion.

Glenn, S. (1988). *Developing capable young people*. Presented at the Minnesota Chemical Dependency Association fall conference, St. Cloud, Minnesota.

Godin, S. (2007). *The dip: A little book that teaches you when to quit (and when to stick)*. New York: Penguin.

Goldsmith, M. (2007). *What got you here won't get you there: How successful people become even more successful*. New York: Hyperion.

Goleman, D. (1998). *Working with emotional intelligence*. New York: Bantam.

Gottman, J. (2012). *Why marriages succeed or fail: And how you can make yours last.* New York: Simon & Schuster.

Grinder, M. (1997). *The science of non verbal communication.* Battle Ground, WA: Michael Grinder & Associates.

Grinder, M. (2000). *The elusive obvious: The science of non-verbal communication.* Battle Ground, WA: Michael Grinder & Associates.

Hammond, S., & Mayfield, A. (2004). *The thin book of naming elephants: How to surface undiscussables for greater organizational success.* Bend, OR: Thin Book Publishing.

Harvey, T., & Drolet, B. (2004). *Building teams, building people: Expanding the fifth resource.* Lanham, MD: Rowman & Littlefield.

Horn, S. (1996). *Tongue fu!: How to deflect, disarm, and defuse any verbal conflict.* New York: St. Martin's Griffin.

Horn, S. (2012). *Tongue fu! Get along better with anyone, anytime.* Knoxville, TN: Cool Gus Publishing.

Horowitz, B. (2014). *The hard thing about hard things: Building a business when there are no easy answers.* New York: Harper Business.

Howell, E. (2019, May 1). Challenger: The shuttle disaster that changed NASA. *Space.com.* Accessed at www.space.com/18084-space-shuttle-challenger.html on June 22, 2020.

Huxley, A. (1933). *Texts and pretexts: An anthology with commentaries.* London: Chatto and Windus.

Johansen, B. (2007). *Get there early: Sensing the future to compete in the present.* San Francisco: Berrett-Koehler.

Johnson, B. (1992). *Polarity management: Identifying and managing unsolvable problems.* Amherst, MA: HRD Press.

Joni, S., & Beyer, D. (2010). *The right fight: How great leaders use healthy conflict to drive performance, innovation, and value.* New York: HarperCollins.

Kahane, A. (2004). *Solving tough problems: An open way of talking, listening, and creating new realities.* San Francisco: Berrett-Koehler.

Kahane, A. (2017). *Collaborating with the enemy: How to work with people you don't agree with or like or trust.* Oakland, CA: Berrett-Koehler.

Kerfoot, K. (2009, July/August). What you permit, you promote. *Nursing Economics, 27*(4), 245.

Keller, G. (with Papasan, J.). (2013). *The ONE thing.* New York: Hachette.

Laborde, G. Z. (1987). *Influencing with integrity: Management skills for communication and negotiation.* New York: Syntony.

Lencioni, P. (2002). *The five dysfunctions of a team: A leadership fable.* San Francisco: Jossey-Bass.

Lencioni, P. (2016). *The ideal team player: How to recognize and cultivate the three essential virtues.* Hoboken, NJ: Jossey-Bass.

Leymann, H. (1990). Mobbing and psychological terror at workplaces. *Violence and Victims, 5*(2).

Leymann.se. (n.d.). *Mobbing is a common issue.* Accessed at www.leymann.se /English/frame.html on June 22, 2020.

Lynch, D., & Kordis, P. (1988). *Strategy of the dolphin.* New York: Fawcett Columbine.

Marshak, R. (2006). *Covert processes at work: Managing the five hidden dimensions of organizational change.* San Francisco: Berrett-Koehler.

Miller, M. (2015). *Chess not checkers: Elevate your leadership game.* Oakland, CA: Berrett-Koehler Publishers.

Murrell, D. (2018). Adrenaline rush: Symptoms, causes, and meaning. *Medical News Today.* Accessed at www.medicalnewstoday.com/articles/322490 on May 24, 2020.

Olsen, W., & Sommers, W. (2003). *A trainer's companion: Stories to stimulate reflection, conversation, action.* Baytown, TX: aha! Process.

Pacanowsky, M. (1995). Teams tools for wicked problems. *Organizational Dynamics, 23*(3), 36–51.

Pascale, R., Sternin, J., & Sternin, M. (2010). *The power of positive deviance: How unlikely innovators solve the world's toughest problems.* Boston: Harvard Business Review Press.

Pfeffer, J., & Sutton, R. (2000). *The knowing-doing gap: How smart companies turn knowledge into action.* Boston: Harvard Business School Press.

Pink, D. H. (2009). *Drive: The surprising truth about what motivates us.* New York: Riverhead Books.

Pope, C. (2016, April 20). Toyota, the 'best built cars in the world'? Ad watchdog not so sure. *The Irish Times.* Accessed at www.irishtimes.com/news/ireland /irish-news/toyota-the-best-built-cars-in-the-world-ad-watchdog-not-so -sure-1.2617540 on January 30, 2020.

Raffoni, M. (2008). Are you spending your time the right way? *Harvard Business Review*. Accessed at https://hbr.org/2008/02/are-you-spending-your-time-the-1 on June 22, 2020.

RAND Corporation. (2007). *Evaluating the effectiveness of pay-for-performance*. Accessed at www.rand.org/capabilities/solutions/evaluating-the-effectiveness-of-teacher-pay-for-performance.html on May 24, 2020.

Ray, S. (2015). *Stevie Ray's improv company*. Accessed at www.stevierays.org on March 9, 2020.

Reina, D., & Reina, M. (1999). *Trust and betrayal in the workplace: Building effective relationships in your organization*. San Francisco: Berrett-Koehler.

Rock, D. (2010). SCARF: A brain-based model for collaborating with and influencing others (Vol. 1). *The NeuroLeadership Journal*. Accessed at https://neuroleadership.com/portfolio-items/scarf-a-brain-based-model-for-collaborating-with-and-influencing-others/ on March 9, 2020.

Rogers Commission. (1986, June 6). *Report of the Presidential Commission on the Space Shuttle Challenger Accident: Chapter V—The contributing cause of the accident*. Accessed at https://history.nasa.gov/rogersrep/v1ch5.htm on May 22, 2020.

Rosenberg, M. (2003). *Nonviolent communication: A language of life*. Encinitas, CA: PuddleDancer Press.

Sala, H. (2016, February 5). You can't give what you don't have. *Guidelines for Living*. Accessed at www.guidelines.org/devotional/you-cant-give-what-you-dont-have/ on May 24, 2020.

Saphier, J., Haley-Speca, M. A., & Gower, R. (2017). *The skillful teacher*. Acton, MA: RBT Publishing.

Satir, V. (1972). *Peoplemaking*. Palo Alto, CA: Science & Behavior Books.

Sheridan, R. (2018). *Chief joy officer: How great leaders elevate human energy and eliminate fear*. New York: Penguin.

Sinek, S. (2009). *Start with why: How great leaders inspire everyone to take action*. New York: Penguin.

Slap, S. (2010). *Bury my heart at conference room B: The unbeatable impact of truly committed managers*. New York: Penguin.

Sommers, W. A., & Zimmerman, D. (2018). *Nine professional conversations to change our schools: A dashboard of options*. Thousand Oaks, CA: Corwin Press.

Stone, D., Patton, B., & Heen, S. (1999). *Difficult conversations: How to discuss what matters most*. New York: Penguin.

Surowiecki, J. (2004). *The wisdom of crowds*. New York: Anchor Books.

Sutton, R. I. (2017). *The asshole survival guide: How to deal with people who treat you like dirt*. Boston: Houghton Mifflin Harcourt.

Sutton, R. I., & Rao, H. (2014). *Scaling up excellence*. New York: Crown.

Violence Prevention Initiative. (2010). *Bullying and harassment in schools*. Accessed at injury.research.chop.edu/violence-prevention-initiative/types -violence-involving-youth/bullying-schools on May 24, 2020.

Waldrop, M. M. (1996). Dee Hock on management. *Fast Company*. Accessed at www.fastcompany.com/27454/dee-hock-management on March 9, 2020.

Wolfe, P. (2010). *Brain matters: Translating research into practice* (2nd ed). Alexandria, VA: Association for Supervision and Curriculum Development.

York-Barr, J., Sommers, W., Ghere, G., & Montie, J. (2016). *Reflective practice for renewing schools: An action guide for educators* (3rd ed.). Thousand Oaks, CA: Corwin Press.

INDEX

Cooper, R., 3
Costa, A. L., 26
credibility, 8, 82
criticism, 12, 32–33, 34
culture of psychological safety, 11,
47, 54, 90

D

data for conflict management, 52
Deci, E., 89
defending yourself strategically,
70–74
defensiveness, 13, 32–33, 34
Developing Capable Young People
(Glenn), 11
deviance, positive, 93–95
The Dip (Godin), 15
distracters, 71, 72, 73
diversity, 6, 9–10
recognizing the value of
opponents and, 99–102
of work styles, 42
Dobson, M., 75
dolphins, 47–49
Dobson, D. S., 75
Drucker, P., 75–76

E

edicts, 7, 24, 107
Edmondson, A., 11, 46
efficacy, 74
"Eight Norms of Collaboration"
(Baker & Shalit), 52
elephants in the room, naming,
52–54
emotions
in affective conflict, 51–52
agile response to, 3–6
calming, 37

civility and, 6, 10–11
countering emotional
blackmail, 58–61
making others feel heard, 66–68
empathy, 35
The Empowered Manager (Block), 100
evaluation and elimination, 114, 116
exaggeration, 23
exceptions, 23
expectations, 1, 51, 77–78, 102
experimentation, 46, 99

F

facilitating controversy, 96–99
facts, 77
fairness, 62, 64–65
fear, 88
The Fearless Organization
(Edmondson), 11
feedback
delivering bad news
productively, 80–83
ratio of positive vs. negative,
35–36
Felps, W., 107–108
*50 Myths and Lies that Threaten
America's Public Schools* (Berliner
& Glass), 89
fight, flight, freeze, or appease
responses, 4–5
fighting the right fight, 119–120
FIT acronym, 119–120
five-fifteen reports, 75
flexibility, 74
Forward, S., 60
framing, 3, 68–70
Fredrickson, B., 36
FRISK model, 76–78
fuzzy language, 19–25

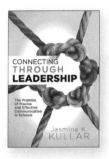

Connecting Through Leadership
Jasmine K. Kullar
The success of a school greatly depends on the ability of its leaders to communicate effectively. Rely on *Connecting Through Leadership* to help you strengthen your communication skills to inspire, motivate, and connect with every member of your school community.
BKF927

Working With Difficult & Resistant Staff
John F. Eller and Sheila A. Eller
Identify, confront, and manage all of the difficult and resistant staff you encounter. This book will help school leaders understand how to prevent and address negative staff behaviors to ensure positive school change.
BKF407

Leading Difficult Conversations
Richard DuFour and Rebecca DuFour
Transforming a school into a professional learning community requires changing behaviors, beliefs, and processes, which can cause resistance and conflict. This video shows how to hold conversations that lead to higher levels of commitment to core PLC practices.
DVF047

Transforming School Culture, Second Edition
Anthony Muhammad
The second edition of this best-selling resource delivers powerful, new insight into the four types of educators and how to work with each group to create thriving schools. The book also includes Dr. Muhammad's latest research and a new chapter of frequently asked questions.
BKF793

a division of

Solution Tree | Press
Solution Tree

Visit SolutionTree.com or call 800.733.6786 to order.

GL🌐BAL **PD**

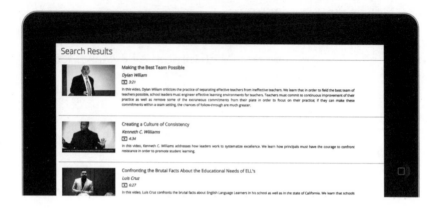

Access **Hundreds of Videos & Books** from Top Experts

Global PD gives educators focused and goals-oriented training from top experts. You can rely on this innovative online tool to improve instruction in every classroom.

- Gain job-embedded PD from the largest library of PLC videos and books in the world.

- Customize learning based on skill level and time commitments; videos are less than 20 minutes, and books can be browsed by chapter to accommodate busy schedules.

- Get unlimited, on-demand access—24 hours a day.

▶ **LEARN MORE**
SolutionTree.com/GlobalPDLibrary

 Solution Tree